Rebirth

YVONNE ELLIOTT

LA2YE Publishng
Chicago, Illinois

Rebirth

YVONNE ELLIOTT

♦ DEDICATION ♦

I dedicated this book to everyone who believed in me when I did not believe in myself. To everyone who used the following phrases, "Get over it," "Shake it Off," "Let it go," "It's in the past, leave it in the past," "Pray on it and give it up to God." Well, guess what? I did all of that, and you know what happened? God gave it back to me and told me that my story needed to be shared with the world. Is this my entire life story? No, but these pivotal points of my life made me who I am and led me to realize that other women in the world may also feel they have it all together on the outside only to feel raw and broken on the inside, and they may need the perspective that I'm able to provide.

This book is for everyone who advised me to build bridges with strong pillars towards a life I was meant to live instead of hopping from rock to rock, only surviving. I dedicate this book to everyone who took the time to encourage me, even when I didn't ask for it. People appear in your life for a reason or a season and will fill in their specific puzzle pieces when the time is right. I am grateful to you, my friends, and my family, my puzzle pieces who helped me create this picture.

I dedicate this book to the people are moving through life as adults with missing pieces from a shattered childhood. Somehow, we hold jobs and raise our own families even though we are not quite whole. May my story show you how to feel complete on the inside despite the pieces you felt were missing as a child. I dedicate this book to those who don't have it all figured out yet, but are trying. Even if we make a mistake or two, we understand we must keep pushing forward, even though the answers are not all there. Finally, I dedicate this book to my village, which served as my pillars growing up. The planks on my bridge to live the life I imagined as a little girl. The life I envisioned in bits and pieces like a broken mirror as a young woman and the life I'm building as an adult. This memoir is my "step out on faith" and the manifestation of my dreams.

"In order to love who, you are, you cannot hate the experiences that shaped you."
~ Andrea Dykstra

♦ ACKNOWLEDGEMENTS ♦

In December 2020, I decided to work on manifesting for one year to see if it would work. In February 2021, a Facebook posting led me to NK's Tribe Called Success. I followed my intuition and entered a writing challenge to help me finish my book. I thought it would be just a couple of people that would keep me motivated and teach me more about the beating in my heart that I'd avoided for so long.

What I found was a writing family, a group of people that not only share a love of writing but share the same vision. From my book coach Shakir, who answered my text messages no matter how basic my questions were. To the editors, beta readers, and designers who worked with me every step of the way. Thank you for your input, recommendations, and love.

Lastly, I'd like to thank Naleighna Kai for believing in me and not giving up on me through this process, even though I might have given up on myself. I passionately believe people are placed in your life for a reason, and she was placed in my life at the right time to help push me towards fulfilling my dream.

Yvonne Elliott

Chapter 1

I'M NOT SUPPOSED TO BE HERE

"Always remember that striving and struggle come before success in the dictionary." — Sarah Ban Breathnach

There was a girl that looked like a rat but blossomed into a chocolate drop and ultimately a phoenix. Her life wasn't easy by any means, but then most tales, the ones that matter, always start that way.

The story is mine, and the chapters within are like puzzle pieces thrown against the fabric of time in many ways. Some fell near my feet like the pieces of my heart. Others I found along the way, like breadcrumbs feeding a soul forever starving for the attention of a mother that chose addiction over me.

Maybe by the end, you will look upon these pages and my past as a map across the dangerous waters of life. Perhaps you will see as the pieces evolve. In the end, the picture may be different from where you started, but just as valuable.

Not all angels have wings. I count myself fortunate to have known not one, but quite a few in my lifetime. I was born to a drug-addicted mother, so the odds were already stacked when I took my first breath. Everyone thought I was bound to have congenital disabilities and emotional and developmental delays.

Combine that with a father who spent most of those early years in prison, and the armchair psychologists had me all figured out— predestined to repeat the mistakes of my parents, unable to learn the simplest of things. To hear them tell it, my breaths and days were numbered. But then, isn't that how a phoenix is made?

They didn't know the band of angels watching out for me. I read somewhere that many of us are here because of a grandmother's prayers. Gigi, Glama, I could go on about the nicknames and terms of endearment that we all give to the family's matriarch, but their mission remains the same. My Grandma's hands were warm with life and a wealth of love for all forty ounces of me.

My first angel came when I was born. Weighing 2.5 pounds at St. Luke Presbyterian hospital in 1980, the fact that I even survived birth is a miracle. I've listened to my grandmother and godmother tell the story many times. The storytelling began at family gatherings, as sunlight, cocoa butter, and barbeque perfumed the air.

Aluminum foil pans of Potato and Macaroni salad joined the bottomless bowls of chips and pretzels on one end of the table. Cake stands filled with all kinds of desert lined another. The faint smell of freshly cut pineapple wafted in the air, indicative of the prized hand-churned pineapple sherbet that ended every family function. Kids my age and older hovered around that table, sneaking fingerfuls of icing before running off to continue a game of freeze tag or another dance contest, all under the watchful eyes of their mothers. I'd walk up, hug, and say hello to my godmother, and she'd respond with,

"You're a pretty little girl." She'd say while shooting a knowing look at my grandmother.

My grandmother often chimed in with, "Yes, she is."

Then my godmother said, "We weren't always sure how you'd look.

When you were first born, you looked like a little rat."

My eyes always lowered when she said that. All I could picture were the little newborn rats I'd seen in my science books in school. Then my grandmother would interject. "Yes, you looked like a little rat when you first came out. You didn't have any hair, no eyelashes, no nothing. Just a little body with a heartbeat and a brain."

"Yeah, like a bald little rat," my godmother said with a chuckle.

"But suddenly…," my grandmother's voice turned sweet. That change in tone was my godmother's cue to nod and agree.

"It's like God took a pencil and started to draw."

"Um-hum," they'd say together.

"Every day, I went to the hospital to see you, and every day it was something new." My grandmother said, "One day you didn't have eyelashes, then I came back, and you had eyelashes. One day no eyebrows, then the next day, eyebrows. Before I knew it, you had a little brown face."

She'd turn to look at me and smile before my godmother chimed in.

"Yeah, the nurses called you 'Chocolate Drop."

Then they hugged me, patted me on the behind, and sent me on my way. Somehow, a micro-preemie born in 1980 survived, but my initial struggles set the stage for many challenges in my life.

Fear for me never came in the guise of a vampire or werewolf or giant as one would find in children's books. Part of me would have welcomed the imaginary one. The real ones made you cry. The human ones made you scream.

Someone broke into our apartment on Lawndale Avenue in Chicago when I was five. With nothing but the clothes on our backs, my mother packed us up and flew us to California. As my mother worked through her issues, we were like nomads, moving from one place to another. I found out later her 'grown up' problems began and ended with an addiction.

Another angel swept into my life on the day a drug dealer severely beat my mother. Since I wasn't old enough to be left home alone during the day, Mom took me with her when she went to score drugs. That day, she sent me to the taco truck with three dollars to get some rolled tacos, a cheap, quick meal. I waited in front of the liquor store, just as my mother had instructed. "Sit right here. Don't talk to anyone you don't know. I'll be right back. What's the secret password?"

"Superman." I said confidently. We'd learned in school about stranger danger and how we weren't supposed to go with another adult unless they knew the secret password.

After a while, fear crept in. It's always there in the back of a child's mind when a parent is late coming to pick them up. Sometimes it creeps in like a nagging feeling. After it happens three or four times, it settles over you like a soggy cloak. My mind began to race.

She forgot where she left me. Did I do something wrong? I must have forgotten to clean up my toys, or maybe I was too loud, and she got so mad that she just left me behind. Maybe she didn't want me anymore. and…and…

Terrifying images built in my head as I craned my neck to see where she had gone. That same wild fear made my heart cramp in my chest as I hurried down the street in the direction she went.

I wasn't a baby anymore. Babies cried. Little girls whined and wiped their noses on their shirt sleeves.

By the time I reached the end of the parking lot, I was in a dead run. She wasn't there. My heart rattled against my ribcage as reality set in. And then, a familiar blue sports car pulled up next to me. The vehicle belonged to a man my mother had befriended.

"Get inside," he barked through the rolled-down window before shoving the front passenger side door open.

I started walking towards the car, then froze. My mother's words rang in my head.

Don't talk to strangers, and whatever you do, never get into someone's car, even if you know them without them knowing our secret password.

"Where's my mom?" I asked, backing away from the car.

"She's the RV up the street. Now come on," he snapped. I looked toward the place he indicated, and there was my mom, covering her face with a shirt.

"Yonne, get in the car with Lars," she ordered before staggering to the RV a few feet away.

"No, I want to go with you," I called as I took a few steps in her direction.

"No, get in the car with Lars. Do as I say. He's going to take you home," she said, wincing as a stranger helped her into the back of the vehicle.

By then, I was crying. "Where are you going?" I whined, not knowing what was going on or what happened.

Lars guided me into the front seat of his car, and we followed the RV as it pulled out onto the main road. Through the back window of the RV, I could see my mother rocking back and forth, still holding that bloody shirt up to her face. We followed the RV until we hit the expressway. We turned, but the RV continued straight.

"She'll be okay, Yonne. Let's get you home to bed," he said, trying hard to keep the smile in his voice, but all I had to do was close my eyes, and my mother, covered in blood, filled my mind.

Lars took me back to the apartment we shared with him. He put me in bed and told me my mother would be all right. When I was scared, I would rock myself to sleep and say a little chant in my head: I'm cold, I'm hungry, and I want my mommy, I'm cold, I'm hungry, and I want my mommy.

The words swirled within me, circling the gaping hole in my heat where my mother should have been. The harder I cried, the more the chant morphed and grew louder than my tears and my heartbeat thumping in my ears as the words swelled in my throat.

I want my mommy, and then I want my granny. I want my granny; I want my granny.

Mercifully, sleep found me, and a dream unfolded where God scooped me up in his arms, flew me to Chicago, and put me in my grandmother's bed, where it was safe, warm, and familiar. I don't know how it happened, but my angel came and got me. The next thing I remember, I was in my grandmother's bed.

Many years later, in my late 30s, I shared that story to my aunt as we piled into my car for a day of running errands. She had the strangest look on her face as tears gathered in her eyes.

"That was me," she said finally before shifting her focus to the rushing traffic.

"Huh?" I asked as I quickly divided my attention between driving the car and watching her stumble over the memories.

"Yonne, that was me; I was the one that came and got you, she said, wincing at some private thought. "We were in the basement doing hair when the phone rang. Your grandmother slumped into the chair with this look on her face. "We got to go get Yonne," she said. "Something happened to Nire, and we got to go get Yonne." My aunt looked at me with tears leaking from the corners of her eyes.

"Baby, Granny, hung up that phone, went upstairs to her room, and came out with some cash. I threw some clothes in a bag and was on my way to the airport on the next flight out to get you."

My eyes welled up with tears. "It was you? You're my angel?" My voice cracked with emotion. "I swear, Tee, I remember nothing that happened from when I was in Lar's car. I don't know how I got back to Chicago or how much time had passed."

When we got to our destination, as soon as we got out of the car, I walked over to my aunt and wrapped my arms around her. Hugging her tightly. I whispered in her ear, "Thank you for saving me."

How could I know that other angels would appear to shelter me from the coming storms in the years to come?

PERSPECTIVE

The actions of one person can change the life of another. Looking back on the people who chose to show up in my life during a time when I needed them, they are some of the most invaluable people in my life. I refer to them as angels because they appeared suddenly and made a way when there seemed to be no other way. Like pebbles dropped in a lake that ripple for miles away, their minor actions changed the tide of everything around them, whether the person realizes it or not.

TOOLS THAT HELPED ME

Faith, through my angels, I've learned how to have faith. The bible describes faith as the substance of things hoped for and the evidence of things not seen. My angels appeared in my life right when it seemed my confidence was running low or had run out. Through their appearances, I've learned how to strengthen my faith muscles. Even when things don't turn out exactly how I'd like them to, I know everything happens for a reason, and when I need help, an angel isn't too far away.

This book is broken into sections. You'll get a tidbit from my life, the perspective I've gained, and the mental tool that helped me get through my issues. I've used these tools one at a time or in combination. Hell, some weeks, I'll use all of them at various points to help me get through.

Chapter 2

RATIONAL/IRRATIONAL

"Elsewhere is a detour on a road paved with grief."
— Stephanie M. Freeman

Liquor before beer and you're in the clear is a favorite rhyme of the drinker. Thankfully, the third angel that came to me looked past the alcohol and found me.

I was new to the Air Force and had learned how to drink like most of my peers. A lot. I drank sailors under the table and didn't blackout, unlike everyone else. One night, I was on the beach, and it was time for us to go home, and since I was the 'most sober,' I drove a car that belonged to the guy I was dating.

We were driving on what is known in Florida as the two-mile bridge. We were about half a mile in when I glanced in my rearview mirror and saw an underage drinker's worst nightmare. The red and blue flashing lights beaming down on us made my friend and boyfriend fall silent. I glanced at the speedometer and made sure I was driving at the speed limit. When I looked in the rearview mirror again, my boyfriend was vomiting dinner chunks out of the rear window. OMG! We are going to jail. I yelled to my friend. "Amy, get his head back into the car. There's a cop behind us."

Amy shouted at our friends in the backseat to comply. As he brought his head in, I prayed silently in my head. "Dear Lord, please, if you get us out of this, I swear I'll never drink and drive again. Like ever."

The cop sped up behind us, lights flashing.

I slowed down a little, but there wasn't a shoulder on the bridge. The cop noticed us slowing down and sped around us to wherever he was going. Oh my God. The cop wasn't chasing us. He was responding to a call, and we were in his way. As the cop sped off, we all sobered up quickly and made it back to the base without incident. Twenty Years later, I never have over one drink if I know I'm going to drive. The promise I made to God that day stuck. I would have been kicked out of the military even before my career started if we had gotten caught. God held his end of the bargain, and I have maintained mine.

The fourth time an angel came was a couple of years later. I wasn't quite twenty-one. I had made it to my first base and settled in but couldn't do my job yet because I didn't have a security clearance. So, I did 'grunt work,' as it's called. I sat at the emergency desk, cleaned weeds, and ran the linen exchange. This went on for months because it takes a little longer to determine if you are a threat to national security when your dad is in federal prison, and your mother had a few short stints in jail of her own.

One Saturday, around six in the morning, my mother called me. I could tell she was high because she talked super-fast. Counselors refer to the fast-talking as raging. "Hey, Yonne."

"Hey, Mom." I rolled my eyes, hating when she called me raging. Because it usually meant she would ask for money I didn't have.

"Hey, I just called to tell you." my mother said in a quick, snappy tone. "Your uncle John's got HIV."

My mind blanked out and returned when she said, "Yup, fucking AIDS. He's in the pulpit preaching to people, and he's about to die."

The air felt as though it had been sucked out of the room, and the world began to spin as I tried to process what she had just said. One of my favorite uncles, the one who bought me candy, talked to me like an adult and asked for my opinions about life and the news and politics. Had HIV? I could not process it.

"I've got to go." I disconnected before she could say anything else and plopped down on the bed. Her tone was matter of fact and condescending, so 'I'm better than your uncle because he has HIV, and I don't. Ha Ha.'

At that moment, I cried, feeling sick, sad, and angry all at the same time. I thought of my grandmother and how she must have felt and my cousins discovering that their father was living on borrowed time. I was too far away from the issue, and even if I was closer, there wasn't a damn thing I could do about it.

Why did she even call me? It wasn't like the life she was leading gave her a pass. One wrong hit and her death could have easily been the topic of conversation.

I couldn't deal. So, what does any young person who receives devastating news do? Hold an alcohol-induced Irish wake of sorts. My uncle wasn't on display in a casket for the world to judge, but the sentiment, at least for me, was about the same. He wasn't even in the grave yet, but there I was, preparing to down anything I thought would blunt the grief and honor the man I remembered. I waited until about 1:00 p.m. and walked down to a friend's room. I knocked on the door and woke him up.

"Hey, we should have a party," I said. "Find me when you get up. I need you to buy me some drinks." My friend didn't know any better. He heard "drinks," and he was ready. Later that night, we picked up some pizza, Mad Dog 20/20, and Boones Farm. Typical party items of choice for the 2000s I didn't have enough ready cash to pay for any of it. I took the money from my savings account. I opened my room door, turned on my stereo, and had a Saturday night party.

Many of my friends came by, and we drank, smoked cigarettes, played video games, and had a good time. That night I drank so I wouldn't feel anything. No sadness. No pain. I wanted the hurt and the anger to go away. On some level, I had convinced myself that drinking would erase my uncle's HIV. The last friend left my room just before dawn. The room was spinning, and the sun hadn't touched the sky. I laid down and fell into a drunken slumber.

When I woke up, I felt dizzy. I closed my eyes and heard my mother's words replaying like a scratched record in my head. Nauseated, I sat up and tried to make it to the bathroom. Unfortunately, the contents of my stomach made it before the rest of me did. In the middle of throwing up on the floor, I cried. Since I shared the bathroom, I had to clean it up before my suite mate saw it. I managed to pick myself up off the floor and slowly started the process of cleaning and crying.

Everything I didn't want to feel came back up in a rush. Why is she like that? How could she tell me like that? Why didn't she just stop? After nineteen years, I was tired of her tone and her words tearing me apart. As I continued to clean, it was like God lifted my head, and as the tears streamed down my face, I realized I couldn't do this. I couldn't continue to deal with my mommy issues by drinking. It was turning me into her, and I was not my mother.

If any action I took resembled something "Nire" would do, I'd do the opposite. I promised myself I wouldn't become a drug addict like her. After that event, I didn't have another drink for six months. My twenty-first birthday came, and I didn't even have the desire to go out and have my first "legal" drink. God sent the fifth angel to protect me again. Only this time, the angel came in the form of my intuition.

PERSPECTIVE

Looking back on the event eighteen years later, I still don't understand why my mother gave me that news in the way she did. She had an illness, and much like a tornado, her destruction was random and without rhyme or reason. This event gifted me with the ability to perform internal checks and balances on my actions. If what I'm about to say or do is anything like my mother would do, I don't do it. I try to have empathy and compassion and not use my tongue to inflict ill will on others.

As far as my angels are concerned, while they are not as apparent as they once were, they're still around — watching, waiting, coming to me in dreams, showing me a glimpse of greatness. Now I understand they are manifestations of what I could become, visions of my future, a small reward for the growing pains I went through. I'm blessed and want to use my experiences to help others. I'm obligated to be an angel for someone else who may need one.

As I told the story about my second angel to my therapist, she asked about my feelings. Why was I shaken by writing it? I explained that those intense fears returned all over again. Like a story playing out in my head, and I didn't know what to do. She asked me, "how can you defuse the uncertainty and fear when they come up today?" I wasn't sure how to answer because, in those moments, I felt like I was nine and not thirty-nine years old. She challenged me to breathe and remember that I can handle whatever comes my way. I'm also able to control more now than I could manage back then. I can step out on faith and know that things will be okay.

TOOLS THAT HELPED ME

Remember to breathe. I know it's bullshit, right? "Breathe through the anxiety. Deep breath in through the nose and out through the mouth." "Whoosah."

This slows your heart rate. Keep breathing until the anxiety goes away. The therapist makes it sound easy, but they don't tell you how that first attempt will feel like you are trying to inhale through chocolate pudding. Thick and damn near impossible. Despite how hard it feels, take a breath. It is the first step towards being mentally free. Imagine that you can get your mind to take that first step. If you can, you are well on your way to more significant actions. So, when you feel that gut punch, the air being sucked from your soul, then take that first breath.

All while knowing that it's cliché. That first exhalation is the breath leading you on the path to living a life for yourself and surviving what currently feels insurmountable. Take the time to remember that you've survived worse things before, and you can survive this as well.

Chapter 3

PRESENCE

"The Strongest Presence is so often an Absence." —Steve Rasnic Tem

Having absentee parents is hard. The stability and security that a child needs growing up is tested and tried repeatedly. One question, which was ever-present in my life, was, "Why didn't you show up?" I frequently asked this question at various childhood points, mainly during school events.

Most kids want to do well in school. From day one, our parents taught us that we need to get good grades and turn in all assignments if we're going to be accepted and held in high regard. When a kid has an absent parent, that child does one of two things: A. Acts out to get attention, or B. Tries to overachieve to gain affection and attention. I chose the latter.

I tried to win as many awards as possible, hoping that my mother would show up for a ceremony one day. Somehow, I decided that she'd stop doing drugs if I got good enough grades. If I got an award big enough that gave me enough exposure, I'd become more important than my mother getting her next hit, and she would choose me. The dream in my head rarely happened.

Usually, the principal would announce my name for whatever award I was winning. I'd walk up on the stage, smile big, take my award and face the audience for the obligatory parental wave, only to find an empty seat and no one to wave at. With my head held high, I hurried off the stage and slumped in the chair, fighting back the tears of disappointment over being forgotten yet again. Once home, I'd find my mother sleeping. I'd shake her and ask, "Where were you? I had my ceremony today. Remember?"

She'd mumble something like, "Oh, that's nice. I'm sorry I missed it. I'll make it next time."

Then she'd roll over and go back to sleep. I slowly turned around with my awards crumpled up in my hand and walked out of the room, throat burning, trying to hold back my tears. Why waste the tears when my mother didn't care?

She showed up to important things like graduations, but her grand appearances always fell flat. Special occasions like birthdays and graduations meant money and late-night visits to my room once the festivities were over. She'd creep into my room in the middle of the night, shake me awake and say, "I know you got some money inside those cards; let mommy borrow five or ten dollars. I'll pay you back when I get my check on the first." Of course, I was never repaid. After a while, I didn't care too much about getting awards at the end of the grading period because it wasn't like anyone would show up to see me receive them.

Although I completed my schoolwork, the desire to excel was long gone by the 7th grade. If I pulled a couple of A's and a few B's, it was good enough to keep my extended family from nagging me and ensured I could have my freedom and, as I got older, keep my job and eventually graduate. The "just enough" mindset carried over into my military career.

I've never wanted to stand out. Winning an award wasn't necessary to me. If I did my job and was reliable, completing the mission suited me just fine.

PERSPECTIVE

My experience taught me not to make promises to kids that I can't keep. I try not to tell my kids I will be somewhere and not show up. My husband and I show up for most events. If they tell us they are performing or winning an award, we are in the front row with a camera ready to record and take pictures.

With every victory, every accomplishment, I was there. When my children turned to face the audience and wave, my husband and I were there smiling and waving every time my parents weren't there for me. One day, my youngest son had an award ceremony and didn't tell us about it. While having dinner, he brought the certificate to the table to share.

"Look, Mom, I got this today," he said with a wide smile; my childhood memories flooded me as I looked at his face.

"That's great, baby. Why did you get the award?"

He said he got it for most improvement in reading. I said, "Wow, that's great! You've been working hard on your reading. Did you get this in class, or was there a ceremony?"

"Oh, I got the certificate during the quarterly ceremony."

I replied, "Why didn't you tell us when it was? Daddy or I would have been there to cheer you on."

"Oh, I didn't think it was that big of a deal," he said. "I figured you guys would be too busy, so I didn't tell you."

That's when I told him that his dad and I would always make time for him and his brother. Everything they win is important to us, and we would show up for them. There have been other times when my youngest son told us he needed us to show up to school for events on days when he needed our "support." His ability to verbalize his needs at such a young age is an accomplishment and a lesson I'm glad my kids understand. It's not enough to "say" you'll show up, but show up and give support, seen and unseen.

TOOLS THAT HELPED ME

Grace, perseverance, and realizing that I have a void in this area has helped me, and it is okay. Discovering that showing up for my children and other children I care about did not fix the gap left, despite all the work I've done piecing myself back together from my brokenness. The area of abandonment still requires the most work. So, the tool that helps me in this area is perseverance.

I keep showing up, even on the days when I doubt myself and question my self-worth or when it gets tied to some type of superficial bullshit. I remind myself that even when I do not feel worthy, there are people in my life that think the world of me. People in my life whose day I made a little brighter. My strategy is to take the hurt from the absence and fill it with a presence in someone else's life. Is it always easy to do? Oh, hell no. But I keep trying and keep giving love and showing up. Because if I don't, the void will consume me, and I don't want that to happen. I recognize circumstances beyond my control will cause me not to show up for my kids. The gut-wrenching guilt used to overwhelm me, but I allow myself grace and understand I am not my mother, and not showing up for one event won't create the same abandonment issues in my children that were etched into me.

Chapter 4

MONEY MATTERS

"Anybody who thinks money will make you happy hasn't got money."
                                                    — David Geffen

Ten years ago, unexpectedly, I called my brother and asked him.

"Hey, do you still hide your money?"

"You know what? I just recently stopped doing that." He said.

"Yeah, me too. How weird is that? I haven't lived around Mom for at least fifteen years, and she passed away ten years ago, and I still hide my money. I still take my wallet and put it in my drawer."

My brother chuckled. "Yeah, I know, I'm married, and I still put my money in a sock in my sock drawer."

The practice of hiding money started years ago when my brother and I were younger. If you live in a house with a parent who has an addiction, money, and things, tend to "go missing." Anything of real value grows legs, never to be found again. I never had a piggy bank since any money I put in became an automatic donation to the "shoot-'em-up dope man foundation." Quarters, nickels, dimes, dollars can all add up to five or ten dollars to buy another hit of drugs.

We all know items we purchase in stores can be returned for money, but do you know the excellent rules we have in place now for when you want to exchange or return an item for cash? Well, things were way more lenient in the late '80s until stores lost too much money through a new way of stealing.

How do I know? Because I was there. I was about six or seven years of age. I was with my mother and one of her friends in California. My mother told me we were going to the mall. "The Mall? We never go to the mall. What's at the mall?"

"Just get in the car," my mother exclaimed. I did as she instructed, and we rode to the mall. We went into JC Penny, but before entering the store, I got the proverbial Black mother speech.

"Look." my mother began. "Keep your mouth shut and don't ask for anything."

"What are we going to buy?" I asked as people passed us on the sidewalk.

My mother said, "Nothing, we're going to return something."

I was confused because neither she nor her friend had anything in either of their hands. But like a good little girl, I did as I was told. I kept my mouth shut as we went into the store and walked to the home goods section. My mother and her friend looked at the sheets; and Mom picked up a set of king-sized ones and showed it to her friend.

"What about this one?" Mom asked.

My mother's friend shook her head. "No, she said, it has to be under fifty dollars to get cashback."

"Okay," Mom said and put the sheets back.

"Here, use this one," Mom's friend said. At that moment, my mother took a balled-up JC Penny bag out of her pocket and put the sheets in the bag. Then we left the back of the store and walked up to the register.

When it was our turn, my mother stepped forward.

"How are you doing?" she said.

My mother's personality and smile drew people in, which is probably why she was the one talking to the saleswoman.

"Hi, I just need to return this sheet set. It turns out it's the wrong color."

Smiling, the saleswoman asked, "Would you like another color?"

"Uh, no, thank you. I'm going to look in a couple of other stores."

"Okay, well," the saleswoman said, "do you have the receipt?"

"Uh, hold on." My mother patted her pockets, acting like she had a receipt.

"Oh no, it's not in my pocket. Is it not in the bag?"

The cashier took the sheets out and shook the bag upside down.

"No, ma'am, it doesn't appear to be in the bag."

"Oh, no." Mom said. "Can I still return them?"

"Oh, it's not a problem, since it is under fifty dollars, you can return them. I just need you to fill out this form, and you'll be on your way." The saleswoman flashed my mother a smile while handing her a small card and an ink pen.

My mother filled out the standard information. Name, address, telephone number, the reason for the return. All of which my mother falsified. I know this since I'd been reading since I was three years old, and mom made sure I understood the address and phone number of whatever houses we stayed in. After filling out the form, the woman opened the register and gave my mother forty-two dollars. My mother took the money and thanked the lady.

As we walked out of the store, my mom and her friend split the money.

"Twenty dollars for you and twenty dollars for me."

My mother gave me two dollars. "Here, Yonne."

I got back in the car and sat back in my seat in disbelief, trying to process what I had just witnessed. My mother just lied and stole from JC Penney. She didn't buy those sheets. We just stole from that store. I spent the rest of the ride to the apartment looking out the rear window, praying the police wouldn't follow us like those car chases in the movies. I just knew we would get caught and go to jail. I was going to jail. For a few weeks after the incident at the store, whenever I saw a police car driving past us, I'd imagine it stopping us on the street and taking us to jail.

As I got older, other amounts of money went missing, birthday money, what little money I earned from sweeping the hair off the floor of my grandmother's salon, change from running to the store to buy milk or more hair supplies. All grew legs and disappeared, but it didn't stop there. Somehow, my first pair of brand-new Nike's went missing about a month after I got them. One night, I left them by the front door, and the shoes grew a whole body and walked away. When I asked about them, my mother denied ever seeing them and made me tear up my room looking for them. After they didn't show up, she said someone took them from me at school, and I didn't report it.

One Christmas, I got a Game Boy. I wasn't the first kid on the block to get one. I was damn near the last. Shortly after my Christmas break ended, it too grew legs. Mom said I took it to school, and the teacher confiscated it. When you grow up like this, you think twice about everything that has value.

Eventually, I didn't want to purchase or have anything of value out of fear my mother would take it away from me. No authentic gold, no name-brand purses, no real jewelry. Why get attached to things when they can end up in the pawnshop? Never to be seen again.

As I grew older, I became more creative with my hiding spots. My money went in my bras, under pillows, inside socks, in the bottom sock drawers, even inside my shoes. It mattered little because when my mother was raging, she would wake me up in the middle of the night and demand to know where the money was, and she wouldn't take no for an answer. She'd leave and come back fifteen minutes later, asking again and again until I gave in and gave up whatever little I had. If I didn't give her my money, something of value would disappear.

When I started working, my grandmother gave me my first course in money management — the family member of addicts edition. The rules required me to get a checking account. She taught me that when I got paid, I needed to deposit my check into the account right away and only have enough cash to buy my bus pass and my lunch money for the week. The rest stayed in the account; she also warned me never to tell my mother what day I got paid.

"Your mom can't take money from you if it's not in the house." She spoke.

This one lesson resonated with me; I'd go straight to the bank and deposit my check on payday. I then would go to the currency exchange right after and purchase a bus pass. After a while, I'd saved enough to make sure I didn't need to be a burden and ask my family for money. My mother took enough for both of us.

PERSPECTIVE

The practice of money insecurity does something to you as a kid. When you grow up without money, it does one of two things: One person goes out and buys everything they can get their hands on out of a sense of deprivation. They must have the best and multiples of everything out of fear of running out of something and not having it for a long time. Or it makes you keenly aware of other people's possessions. It humbles you and makes you notice those things are unnecessary for a well-balanced life. I'd like to think I've grown into the latter since most of the name-brand items I own, my husband either insisted I buy, or he's purchased for me.

Nowadays, I've gotten comfortable not having to hide my money. Still, now and again, I revert to putting my loose dollars and change into a spot where they can't mysteriously grow legs and walk away. Why save money when someone could steal it? Why value money when money purchased drugs and drugs caused so much pain in my life? It is hard to understand the actual value of a dollar when you watch much of it go up in smoke.

Saving for the future and financial planning is non-existent when money doesn't have value. Survival is the name of the game, and leftover funds went to buy things to make everything seem okay on the outside.

TOOLS THAT HELPED ME

Exposure therapy, yes, I said exposure therapy. After moving into my apartment and feeling comfortable, I stopped hiding money. When I noticed the habit of hiding money in my sock drawer or in between, my pillowcases crept in. I'd stop myself and say, "What are you doing? No one will come in here in the middle of the night and ask you for your money."

Then I would place my money in a more normal spot. Like in my wallet, I'd put the wallet on top of the dresser within my eyesight. Once I was comfortable with that. I placed a change jar on my dresser out in the open. I'd check the cup twice a day to see if the change was still there. I've also gotten more comfortable purchasing pricier things for myself on special occasions, like my birthday or after a significant accomplishment. Even though the self-talk through exposure therapy still exists, the feelings are not as strong. I have kept that monster at bay.

Chapter 5

MEMORIES

"I hate getting flashbacks of things I don't want to remember." — Unknown

Addiction is the only disease I know where feeding the darkness satisfies the addicted, but it starves the people surrounding it. Kids are supposed to be kids. They should run, jump, play and grow in an environment that feels safe, but that's not always the case. There are a lot of things kids shouldn't know about or see.

I know what a crack pipe looks like. I know it's made of glass, and cotton goes inside. The rocks go on top and are burned. I know what it smells like when it's burned; it smells like burning plastic mixed with hot metal. Even now, thirty-plus years later I know the smell. I recognize it if mixed between weed, incense, perfume, or sex. I know it. I learned that smell when I was seven years old. It's burned into my mental recesses. The smell is a trigger, and much like the bullet of a gun, it shoots me back to a time when I was young and vulnerable.

Before the day I saw the pipe pressed to my mother's lips, I'd never been able to connect its smell to anything specific. We were in California at this point in my life. We'd moved from two cousins' houses. The first was from my Aunt Lydia's house. She said my mom had to go because she broke into the back of a decorative slot machine kept in her living room. It was full size and lit up and held quarters inside. It would light up and show you three bars, three cherries, or three bells, just like a real slot machine when you pulled the arm. If you got three of a kind, you won some quarters out of the machine. My mother waited until Aunt Lydia left the house and found some way to pry off the back of the machine and take all the quarters out.

A couple of weeks later we moved into my Aunt Jennifer's house. She had four other kids, three girls, and a boy. Three of the kids were older than me, and one was younger. I played with the younger girl the most since we were close in age. I don't remember why we moved from her house. At the time, we lived in California long enough that my mother qualified for state benefits. She could get a cheap apartment under Section 8 and food stamps.

We moved into an apartment complex right up the street from where my Auntie Jennifer lived. It was a two-bedroom, and I had my own room, just like when we were at home in Chicago. My mother quickly befriended a woman who lived in the complex. She had two daughters. One was my age, and the other girl was older. They lived in a two-story townhouse. It was the first time I'd ever seen a townhouse before, and when we first visited, I had fun running up and down the stairs. The girls shared a room, and the younger girl had tons of Barbie dolls and a dream house. I thought it was so cool since most of my toys I left in Chicago.

One evening, my mom told me we were going over to their house for a while. I was excited to go because that meant I didn't have to play in my room by myself, which I did a lot since my mom slept all the time. We went over there, and I was upstairs playing. After a while, it was getting late, and I wanted to go home, so I went downstairs and told my mom. She was busy drinking 40 oz of Old English Beer and smoking. She waved me away and sent me back upstairs.

After a time, the girl's mom came up and told us to get ready for bed.

I didn't have any pajamas, so she told her daughter to give me some; she did, and I got on the bed to go to sleep, but the younger girl kicked me in the bed and was being mean. I cried and wanted to go home.

I got off the bed and crept down the stairs to tell my mom, but as soon as I opened the bedroom door, I smelled something burning; slowly, I went down the steps calling my mom's name, hoping she would hear me and meet me on the stairs. There was loud music playing, and it was smoky. As I went further down the stairs, I could hear popping, crackling inhalations, and adults talking with lungs full of smoke.

"Mom," I called as I crept down one stair.

"Mommy,"

I called again as I crept down another stair. Still no answer. Once I reached the bottom stair, all I had to do was peer around the corner. My eyes burned from the smoke in the room. I poked my head out, and I saw my mom with a pipe up to her face.

"Mom!" This time I raised my voice.

When she looked at me, her eyes got big. Then her friend turned around and saw me. Mom took the pipe from her mouth and coughed.

"Yonne!" she yelled, "go back upstairs!

I tried to go back the way that I came, but I was stuck. I began sobbing with my face in my hands.

"No!" The girls are mean to me; I'm ready to go home."

She quickly came to the stairs. "We're almost ready to go home, just a little while longer," she said

"But Mom, they are mean to me; I can't sleep."

"Okay, baby, I'll talk to them." She walked me back up the stairs and told the girls to be nice to me so we could go to sleep.

Once my mom shut the door, the older girl threw a pillow at my head, "Here, blackie, you can sleep on the floor like a dog!"

I thought about going back downstairs, but I feared what I might see. So, I did what I thought was the lesser of the two evils. I took the pillow and laid it on the floor. There wasn't any carpet, just hard tile. I curled up into a ball and tried to fall asleep, but it was cold, and I didn't have a blanket.

That was the second time I found my happy place. I closed my eyes

and imagined I was home in Chicago, in my grandmother's bed. I started
my chant, "I want my granny, I want my granny, I want my granny," and
rocked myself to sleep on that cold floor. A while later, mom woke me
up and took me home. Once we got there, I told her what the girls had
done to me and said I didn't want to be around them anymore.

PERSPECTIVE

Soon after that, the woman and my mom weren't friends anymore.
Even though I didn't see them again, the smell and the vision of Mom
with a crack pipe never left me. That was the first time I realized why
my mom slept during the day but stayed up all night. I didn't know what
she was smoking, but I knew it did terrible things to her. That was the
first time I felt alone and afraid. I didn't feel safe anymore; my idea of
safety and security was destroyed. I didn't trust her to take care of me
and realized I needed to figure some things out independently.

TOOLS THAT HELPED ME

This might not be the most helpful advice in the world but the one
tool that helped was compartmentalization. As I got older, I got good at
placing things into mental boxes in my brain, and I'd gaslighted myself
into thinking that what I saw wasn't real. Sometimes, if you squint your
eyes hard enough, you can almost see what should've been instead of
what is. Unfortunately, even the best of memories fray at the edges, and
when seen through the eyes of a child, the edges rarely matter. Using the
boxes in my brain allowed me to make mental space for other things.
I made space for joy, love, and hope. As a result, I'm pretty optimistic.
The memories come out from time to time, but when they do, there's no
space for them, so they're unable to take over my brain, enabling me to
navigate them mentally.

Chapter 6

SANTA'S NOT REAL

"Childhood is often the casualty of reality." — Stephanie M. Freeman

Like many young kids, I believed in Santa. When I lived in my grandmother's house, Santa was very real, and he came at midnight. Santa would bring presents and toys and food and candy. It was one of the few times of the year I got new clothes or something that wasn't a hand-me-down. Christmas meant no arguments. Christmas was Mom's presence. Christmas was fun. My family would make the kids go to bed at eight o'clock.

When it got closer to midnight, the house got louder. The doorbell would ring, and laughter would begin. My aunts and uncles would come by and drop their goodies off under the tree. By midnight, my grandmother's small tree had so many gifts. They had spilled off the table top they sat on and onto the floor. It was a remarkable sight. The tree with its red and green twinkling lights. Presents covered with colorful paper, end tables, and coffee tables filled with chips, nuts, and candy bowls.

When I woke up, I'd run down the stairs and go around the large dining room table, kissing family members as I made my way to the tree. The gifts from Santa were unwrapped: toy kitchens, barbie dolls, and tea sets. My eyes grew large when I saw all the things Santa had brought to me. Even though Santa didn't get it right all the time, I still enjoyed my toys and stayed awake until two or three in the morning, playing with my gifts. The commotion would die down about four when everyone went home, and my relatives fell asleep in the house. The following day, my grandmother made us a late breakfast. We dressed in our Christmas best and rode twenty minutes away to my godmother's house for Christmas dinner.

Out of all the wonderful memories I have of Christmas, the one year that stands out to me is the year I realized Santa wasn't real. I was probably one of the last believers at the ripe old age of ten, but until then, I had no reason to doubt he existed. He always came through. Shortly after I moved back to Chicago, my dad went to prison.

That year when I went to see Santa, he asked me what I wanted for Christmas. I said a microscope and wanted to see my dad. I didn't tell Santa my dad was in jail; I just said I wanted to see him. That year on Christmas Eve, when I came downstairs, my dad was sitting there on the sofa, holding a microscope. He helped me put it together, and we sat up all night looking at bits of family members' hair and saliva. It was the best Christmas ever.

Early the following year, my dad went back to jail, and I was told he would be there for a long time. I did not understand what he did or why, and I asked no one for a reason. I just knew that's where he was. Christmas came around again, and I was almost eleven- too big to sit on Santa's lap, but I wanted to see my dad; I wanted him home for Christmas. When Santa asked me what I wanted, I leaned over and whispered into his ear, "My dad is in jail, and I want him to come home for Christmas."

Santa's face dropped, then he sighed and said, "I'll see what I can do."

In my young mind, that was it; Santa would fix it. He was going to have my dad show up for Christmas. When Christmas Eve came, I fell asleep, hoping for a repeat of last year. I was praying I would wake up, and Dad would be downstairs waiting for me. I woke up at 12:01 and ran down the stairs. Dad wasn't there, and my heart sank. I went on like normal, opening my family's gifts. Whenever the doorbell rang as another family member showed up for Christmas Eve fun, I prayed it was him at the door, but it wasn't. When I woke up the following day after all the fun, the phone rang, it was my father. "Hey Dad, I missed you last night. Where were you?"

"I told you, I am in jail, Yonne."

"I know, Dad, but last year you were in jail too, but you made it home for Christmas, and I just thought…" my voice trailed off, and hot tears formed in my eyes. "I thought you'd make it home."

"Oh, Yonne," my dad said with a heavy sigh. "Look, I don't know what your grandmother or your momma told you, but I'm going to be in here for a long time, sweetie. Ain't no getting out of here unless I break out or snitch, and I ain't doing either."

"But I want to see you," I said, tears running down my face. I asked my dad if he would make it home this year.

He said not this year, "I won't be home for a long while."

After I got off the phone, I went upstairs and cried. Santa lied; he did not do what he promised he'd do; he didn't bring my dad home. Santa wasn't real.

I might not have unwrapped my dad that year, but I did receive a box, a mental one, and it's where I placed my dad. My relationship with him for the next nineteen years comprised weekly phone calls, letters, and seasonal visits. Even though my stepmother did her best to make us feel connected, the disconnect was still very real.

PERSPECTIVE

Everyone finds out Santa is not real in their young lives. Some say it is a rite of passage to discover his nonexistence. It's when fairy tales get pushed outside the realm of possibility and are placed firmly in the library's children's section. It's when children lose a part of their innocence. For me, this experience framed how I raised my kids. As I got older, I vowed not to push mythical creatures on my kids: no Santa and no Easter Bunny. I'm not a heartless mother; I still allowed the tooth fairy because, in my mind, the tooth fairy was the only one you didn't have to lie about when it was time for them to stop showing up. Eventually, you stop losing teeth, and the Tooth Fairy stops coming. No reason to lie about their existence to an unsuspecting kid.

Christmas is still magic; it is still my favorite holiday. I bake cookies with my kids and neighbors. We pick out the largest tree we can fit in the house. We decorate big time, wrap, and open presents. The kids and husband get brand new pajamas, and I make a big breakfast on Christmas morning. Equipped with cinnamon rolls, grits, and fruit. We teach our kids the blessing of Jesus and how we share our gifts with others and use the time to reflect on how blessed we were over the year. We just celebrate without the lie of the big fat man that comes down the chimney.

When a parent lies to a child to "protect them" or make them believe what they say or saw wasn't a reality to protect the adult or situation, it's not beneficial; it's detrimental. I realize I value security, and I appreciate the known. My husband says I have a script of how I envision things in my head. If I have an illusion of control, I maintain my security. Mentally, I plan and already see what my next year will look like. It keeps me calm and helps me move through my day without anxiety.

Without a plan, I can't see "it." Whatever "it" is, it makes me uneasy. Even if the plan changes, just having a soft plan gives me something to grasp on to. But what I've learned is that when I plan, God laughs. And not just a little "Tee he he" Yonne's plan is cute, "let-me-jack this-up" laugh, but a full belly, fat man laugh. It's like God's saying, "Oh, okay, let me just jack all this up for you, Yonne, since you keep thinking you have control."

As far as my relationship with my father, I've realized I still relate to him as if he's in prison. Even though he's physically accessible, it's easier for me to keep him contained in a box in my heart. Releasing him out of the box and wishing for the relationship I needed as a ten-year-old is detrimental to our current father-daughter relationship. It hurts and makes me miss the connection I yearned for as a kid. I've learned to love him from afar and love him where he is emotionally, instead of hoping for a past that wasn't meant to be.

TOOLS THAT HELPED ME

As I've grown older and more mature in my life and marriage, I learned to let go of my expectations for my journey. After many a self-help book, I've also come to realize that the journey of life may not look like I envisioned it, even though I still reach the destination. How do I deal with this? I still plan, but I use a pencil and carry a big eraser instead of putting things down in ink. I assess what I do and don't have control over in a situation, and I make the best of what I can touch. If something is outside of my reach, I pray on it or put it out in the universe, exercise patience, and let go. The common phrase for this is "Let go and Let God." I can't believe how many times I've done this where I've wanted something to happen. Still, it wouldn't happen according to my timeline, so I'd pray or focus on it daily for a few days and then let it go. After a while, the plan I envisioned happened, and it was even better than if I'd planned it out and made it happen on my own.

Chapter 7

LARGER THAN LIFE

"I am what is mine. Personality is the original personal property."
— Norman O. B

My mother's personality was larger than life. She commanded every room she walked into and knew most of the surrounding people. Mom could work a room; she smiled at everyone, told just the right jokes, and could hold a cigarette between her lips and talk with the best of them. Sometimes I felt it was all a lie, cause behind that glowing personality and sparkling smile was something else I couldn't identify. Was it sadness, grief, guilt, or anger?

Very few saw the other side of her, which is why I shrank so much. Her personality was so big. I didn't want to break the lie of her positive image to our extended family — from the outside looking in — everything was always excellent. She had the best relationships with those closest to her and did what she was supposed to do. She took excellent care of her kids and gave them exactly what they needed.

They did not know or see the other stuff, the drug-induced rages, the screaming, tears, and begging. The days she spent sleeping, the missed responsibilities during the daytime because she was up all night like a vampire—her inability to get and keep a steady job. I never spoke about it, never let it out, told no one. Why would anybody believe me when on the outside everything seemed okay? Not wanting to peel back the onion just to see some form of decay.

Why would anything change if it was functioning "just so"? Always just one step away from falling apart. Everyone saved her for so long and prevented her from hitting rock bottom. Maybe they did it for my brother and me to keep us from realizing the worst. Perhaps people did it because they felt terrible for the shining light that beamed so brightly, with so much potential and promise. She was just one prayer away from fixing, one more hit away from it being enough, one more rehab away from becoming normal—one five-dollar bill away from things being all better, just one more.

I prayed for the day my mother would wake up, prayed for the day she would understand that we needed her, prayed for her to show up. I prayed for her to shine bright in my life as she did in everyone else's. My unanswered prayers became defiance, spun around to obedience by my grandmother. Her calm requests turned me from ragged anger into soft kisses. Later, while navigating my way, I understood I had a choice. Keep engaging in destructive behavior and wake up just like her or show restraint to prove I was better. I walked a fine line between normal and not normal, dipping my toe into forbidden waters occasionally to see if it would turn me into my mother.

My mother's larger-than-life personality taught me there's a way to make people pay more attention to your character than your complexion. People get so hung up on physical things they cannot take time to look beyond the surface. I've said before that my mother commanded a room. But she also had a way to connect with people, to show them she loved them. To provide laughter and light, even when the moment seemed dark and hopeless.

Everyone is not blessed with the ability to give light. My grandmother has it, my mother had it, and I have it. It's the ability to provide calm and a reprieve no matter what is going on; it can temporarily provide an environment of love and light and joy against an unfriendly world. Even though my mother couldn't love me the way I thought I needed, she could provide that to others, which was her gift to the world.

PERSPECTIVE

My comparative suffering nearly cost me my life. Refusing to talk about the pain I held inside because it didn't seem as bad as someone else's. Yes, I grew up with a drug-addicted mother and a father in prison, but I wasn't raped. I never spent an entire night out on the street, and I never wore dirty clothes. Most of the time, my mental noise is positive. I'm #blessed and #grateful. I've grown up; made it out. I am doing better than my parents. Then the negative voices in my head would start.

'Who do you think you are to think you have issues?' It could always have been worse.' 'Save the therapist's couch space for people with actual issues.'

'Black women are "strong." God saved you. Don't focus on the past; it prevents you from seeing the good in the future. Push It down, lock it away, focus on the good, project the good. Show light and love; be light and love. Oh, and don't forget to smile. You always look so much better when you wear a smile.'

While I've dealt with moments of sadness, I'm not depressed in the clinical sense. However, I still fight those battles today, trying to understand my subtle demons. Though not as damaging on the outside, they still rip apart my insides. They appear as broken promises, filling my life with superficial things, trying to stuff away pain, and avoiding people. Looking for love, unbelievable approval from those with shallow hearts. Unable to receive criticism to become better.

My therapist explained I need to build bridges to live the life I want to live, but how can I do that when I've only seen bridges constructed of match sticks that can catch fire at the smallest clap of thunder? How do I know the bridge I build won't do the same? I'm reminded of the woman at the wailing wall, crying out for Jesus to save her. Lord, stop these tears raining inside me; it's getting soggy here.

Now I've figured out that everyone walks a fine line. The line between functioning and workaholic. The shopaholic and gambler. The overeater and sex addict all walk this line between function and destruction. Some people maintain their balance better than those you see falling apart throughout life. Is everyone one step away from being caught? When does the balancing act end? When is the show over? Are we wrong to believe everyone has a perfect life except for us? Instead of pretending like the grass is greener, why not admit that most of us have demons and are trying to figure this out. Maybe if we were more open about the secrets, we could seek help, heal, and grow.

TOOLS THAT HELPED ME

Defining and learning about comparative suffering opened doors for me. For the folks in the back, comparative suffering is when people try to make sense of their pain by comparing it to other people's pain. Comparative suffering does two things, it allows you to gain perspective, but it also can lessen your feelings, preventing you from dealing with your pain. Once I understood the root cause of my thinking, I could call out the voices when they showed up.

By recognizing that my experiences were mine, I stopped gaslighting myself into thinking that my experiences didn't shape me into who I am without feeling bad about it. I had to admit that it's okay to hold and process the feelings associated with my experiences. These experiences shaped me; they made me; they are me. I permitted myself to open the gates.

I opened Pandora's box. I'm going to be honest. It's not fun, but you have to practice expectation management. Since I expected the process would suck, I could brace myself for the emotions when they showed up. Visualize a pressure cooker. The feelings are bubbling inside, and the timer is about to go off. Knowing where the reactions are coming from allows you to turn on the slow release and let the emotions come out. It gives you the illusion of control over the situation while also dealing with the pain. There is a catch, though. If you choose to process the emotions slowly, you cannot lie to yourself and stop the release. No, take-backs. Promise yourself that you're going to deal with it. Knowing that relief, joy, and happiness are the other side of the release.

Chapter 8

The Taunting

"Whatever words we utter should be chosen with care, for people will hear them and be influenced by them for good or ill." — Buddha

Kids can be cruel. Some are like sharks relishing the blood in the water. Others paddle, desperately looking for the shore. If they are lucky, they survive the day. And then there are the days when the shore disappears, and the sharks begin to feed.

I was bullied as a kid. Not a song here or there or books knocked out of my hand bullied. I mean knock-down, drag-out, no matter where I went, I couldn't escape the torment of being bullied. Kids are killing themselves today for the stuff they bullied me about in the 80s. Bullies single out kids that are too skinny, too fat, too short, too tall, too rich, and too needy. Pick a feature or attribute, and kids will happily weaponize it for you.

It was no different from the mid-1980s to the mid-1990s when I was seven, till the end of my freshman year. Eight years of taunting, torment, fighting, crying, and running. I was picked on before then, but it didn't matter because I was too young to care. However, somewhere around the age of seven, it counted. My first memory of bullying came when I used to walk back and forth from my house to the corner store to pick up one thing or another. I can remember walking to the store happy because I got to keep the change and buy candy. As I skipped down the street, chewing gummy worms and slinging an onion inside a bag around in a circle. I heard voices calling my name.

"Yonne," I turned and saw four boys sitting on the porch

"Hey, Yonne, come here."

I turned back to the house I had walked past.

When I got to the spot on the sidewalk, I stopped in front of the boys on the porch.

"What?" I asked.

"We want to know, why you so dark?" one boy asked.

It was an odd question; I didn't have an answer. I was Black, so why did it matter if I was darker than them.

"Uh, I don't know, I just am," I replied, shrugging my shoulders.

Then it started.

"I know why she's so dark, 'cus she got left out in the sun too long," one boy said.

"Yeah, it's like somebody put you in the oven and forgot to take you out on time," the other boy said.

They all started laughing.

"Yeah, you so dark, you burnt." The first boy chimed in again.

"Yeah, like burnt toast, no wait, bacon." The second boy said.

"Yeah, that's it, burnt bacon," the third boy added.

They all laughed again. I rolled my eyes and turned around to walk away.

"Hey, wait, come back, Yonne. No, wait, Yonne." When I didn't stop, he yelled.

"Burnt bacon, come back!"

"Hey, hey, come back. It's not meat. It's bacon!" the first boy said, "Burnt Bacon!"

They laughed loudly as I continued on my way. I started running towards my house to get away from their voices. If I couldn't hear them, the laughing would stop. I ran home that day, thinking they would forget my new nickname and never repeat it. But it didn't stop. If there were a group of people on the porch, the boys would start the joke again to make everyone laugh. If I could avoid them, I wouldn't hear them since they lived on the other end of the block, and if I couldn't listen to them, I felt safe.

"Hey, look who it is, everybody! It's burnt bacon!" The boys kept screaming, and everyone on the porch laughed at my expense. It was funny to them, but not to me. The most hurtful thing about my new cruel nickname is that the people who gave me this colorful name were black. Some of them were of the same complexion. I knew a little about racism, but I didn't understand colorism. Back then, no one talked about it.

That's the funny thing about knowledge. If we're lucky as we grow older, we learn more about the world and our view and try to make changes to prevent past mistakes. If not, we repeat the previous hurts, like a broken record that won't move to the next song.

One day after running past the hateful boys on my way home from school, I asked my mom, "Why do they make fun of me?"

"They make fun of you because they aren't as pretty as you are," she said. "They make fun of you cause they ain't you." Then she added, "They're jealous of who you are, a cute little dark girl with a big smile."

I smiled, and I went to my room. Later, I thought about what my mother said. They make fun of me because they're jealous. I thought that makes no sense; why would someone make fun of someone who has something they want? I didn't understand. I just wanted to be left alone; I wanted to play.

That summer, my brother came from Mississippi to visit. During the school year, he lived there with his dad but spent the summers with us. I liked it when he visited. He was tall like a giant and would put me on his shoulders and walk me the length of the block. On his shoulders, no one would bother me. Up there, the bullies would leave me alone. I could even go down the block and sit with him on the bullies' porch, and no one called me burnt bacon. The bullies knew better. My big brother would beat them up for messing with me.

Everything felt right until he left town. Then the bullying started again; the bullies' weapons of torment changed with the seasons. I ran from eggs they'd throw at me the week of Halloween. Snowballs once the snow hit the ground; Ice balls as the snow melted. I liked the days when it was too cold, rainy, or snowy for anyone to be outside. I could walk past the house and not hear or see the bullies. They were inside, staying warm.

Spring brought flowers and bullying season.

"Yonne! Come here!" the bullies would yell. If I ignored them, they got louder. "Hey! Burnt bacon! You hear us calling you. Come here!"

I'd cross the street and run home, where I felt safe.

That was till the taunting showed up next door. One spring day, I was outside playing Double Dutch with the girls my age, and someone messed up turning the rope. Turning the rope correctly was a big deal. You had to turn the ropes right, or you couldn't play. I was turning the ropes, and one girl jumped in the rope and missed, then she blamed it on me.

"Why can't you turn right. Burnt Bacon. Dang. "She rolled her eyes and stepped out of the rope, flipping her ponytails.

"It wasn't my fault; you stepped on the rope." I said, "I ain't do nothing. You can't jump and don't call me burnt bacon!" I yelled back at the girl.

Just then, she grabbed the rope from me. "You can't play anymore. Go home, blackly black!"

The other girls bent over, laughing. I stomped my foot and marched up the steps of my porch into the house. I ran into the bathroom, slammed the door behind me, and cried. It wasn't my fault. Why did the girl have to call me Burnt Bacon? It wasn't my name.

Why did I have to be so dark? Why couldn't I be brown? I hated my skin color; it brought me so much pain. Right then, I thought, maybe there was something in the bathroom that could make me lighter. I searched through the many bottles and tubes in the cupboard. We only had soaps and lotions. I thought none of these would work. If I just had the right ingredients, maybe I could scrub the darkness off.

Later that night, at bath time, I ran the water so hot steam was coming off the top, put dish soap in the tub, and tried to get in, but I couldn't even sit in the water. So, I slowly put my feet in as I got used to the temperature of the water; I took a deep breath and looked up to the ceiling. I noticed a small nail brush on the tub's ledge as I gazed downward. I picked it up, examined it, and rubbed it over my body.

I scrubbed my feet first. As I did, some dirt came off, and I thought they "looked" lighter. 'It's working,' I whispered to myself, 'the blackness is coming off.' A smile spread across my face as I lowered myself into the hot water and continued to scrub my legs. Dirt came off them too. Then I looked over to the edge eyeing the container of scouring powder we used to clean the tub with when we were finished bathing. If a brush worked this well, adding cleaner would work twice as well, this stuff cleans everything.

I felt excited and scrubbed faster. I thought this was it; I would no longer look like burnt bacon. They'll finally leave me alone. I scrubbed my entire body with that nail brush, including my face and neck. When I finished, the water was cloudy, and I felt satisfied. I pulled the plug in the tub and washed all of that "blackness" down the drain. After I dried my body off and cleaned the tub, I stood and looked at my face in the mirror. My image was the same; I was just as dark as when I started. Only now, I was ashy, too, since the scouring powder and scrubbing my body dried out my skin. It didn't work. I couldn't wash away the darkness. It was then that I realized I'd have this dark complexion my entire life.

I slowly lotioned my body, put on my pajamas, then came out of the bathroom. My grandmother was sitting at the kitchen table.

"Hey baby," she said, "How was your bath?"

"It was fine," I said as I walked past the kitchen and up the stairs.

No one knew what I was going through and how I felt. I was alone.

PERSPECTIVE

People ask how does it start? How does one begin to hate themselves and start a journey of self-harm? My self-hate started small, comparing my complexion to my family and classmates and looking at my baby pictures to see when the color change started—believing what the kids said. Maybe I was left out in the sun too long; if I stayed inside, would I get lighter? These small notions grow into larger mental lies and bigger changes. It involved hiding behind others, keeping my mouth shut, and making myself as small as possible to stay out of the crosshairs of those looking for a target.

In my dreams, I could shrink. I'd make myself small and travel under the covers, climbing the peaks and valleys of the bed sheets all night chanting prayers to the heavens in hopes of staying that way. Alas, upon dawn's arrival, I'd be back to my normal size left to navigate the world again.

Others deal with it differently; some use bleaching creams and plastic surgery to hide what they don't like about themselves. I'm blessed I didn't have the financial means to change myself, who knows what I'd look like. I've always said God hasn't made me a millionaire yet, because he knows I wouldn't act right. The statement is true in this case because having the means could've been the end of me.

TOOLS THAT HELPED ME

My grandmother says trouble doesn't last always, and over the years, trouble in the form of the kids who used to bully me didn't last. Some of them moved away, and the taunting changed shapes. But as I grew up, I understood that the skin I'm in is all I have, and no matter how much I didn't like it right now, I hoped, much like trouble, that it wouldn't last always.

Chapter 9

THE CRITIC

"There is only one way to avoid criticism: Do nothing, say nothing, and be nothing." — Aristotle

An old saying is framed on a wall in a friend's office. "People who repeatedly attack your confidence and self-worth are quite aware of your potential even if you are not."

I'd love to tell you that the bullying from my narrow-minded color-struck schoolmates stopped, but it didn't. The heckling started again shortly after I started at Dever. The ringleader was the worst kid in the school, K.C. Burns. He was this short, brown boy whose clothes always looked dirty. He caused trouble by talking back to the teachers every day. One day during gym class, he asked.

"Why you talk like that? You sound like dem white kids; what you think you white or something?"

"No, I lived in California before I moved here, and it's how everyone talks there," I said he my face started getting hot. He started, mocking me, putting his hand up with his pinky in the air.

'I lived in California. It's how everyone talks there.'

"That ain't true, you just think you better than e'rr body else, but you ain't better dan me, and you ain't white. You as black as we are."

One of the Black girls sitting next to him started shaking her head in agreement.

"Why dey call you Yonne, anyway? Is it short for yawn cause you so boring?" He smirked. The other kids laughed.

"No," I said, "they call me Yonne cause it's shorter than Yvonne."

"Oh, they need to call you something else." He smirked, then added

"They need to call you skillet." The other kids laughed.

"Yeah, cause you look like my grand momma's cast-iron skillet, black and burnt."

The other kids laughed again. My eyes welled up with tears as I walked away. It was happening all over again, the teasing and turmoil. He got the other kids in on it too. But only the Black and Brown kids participated. The White kids paid no attention. I soon noticed the taunting stopped when he was suspended from school. When he wasn't around, I didn't have to deal with him in class, so all I had to do was survive the bus rides back and forth to school.

I became friends with the other girl on K.C.'s radar. Her name was Ashley, and she had a prominent forehead, so the bullying was distributed between the two of us. The other kids who rode the bus were older and didn't bother us too much, but when K.C was on the bus, he started his hurtful comments. Then the older kids would join in as well. Ashley and I bonded on that bus, ignoring them while whispering to each other what we would do if we looked different.

The taunting changed when I went to high school. What started as comments about my complexion turned sexual into my teens. Again, I wasn't called by my name but by my physical attributes. By the time I was fifteen, I'd awakened with D cup sized breast. It was as if my name changed from Burnt Bacon to Sexual Chocolate overnight. If I wore anything that made my chest stand out, I got attention from the bravest boys who wanted to "date me" to make it to second base. Rarely did any boy look me in the eye. They only looked at my chest.

They weren't interested in my face or hair, just my body. During my freshman year of high school, I joined the gymnastics team. Once the boys found out we'd be flipping around in leotards, and our breasts and thighs would be on display. The bleachers during the home meets were packed with eager teenage boys waiting for a chance to see the girls on display. When the school cut the gymnastics funding at the end of my sophomore year, I was upset and happy. I was upset that I couldn't perform my favorite sport anymore but happy because it meant no more tight leotards, and my boobs were no longer on display.

I could easily hide my chest under sports bras, overalls, and flannel shirts. But when I wore other clothes, there'd always be one boy who came behind me, put his arm around my shoulder, and tossed something down the front of my shirt, causing me to yell and jump around trying to get it out. In this little game, the successful ones like me knew to turn their bodies towards a locker to pull out the rogue object, throwing it at the irritated teenage boy. The unsuccessful girls gave a show for all to see. Sometimes even a random boob would pop out. My nicknames became variations of sexual undertones; Action Jackson, Ms. Jackson if you are nasty, Sexual Chocolate, Sexy. Never beautiful, cute, or pretty.

The first man to tell me I was beautiful was my husband. When he said it, it threw me for a loop. I told him he was the first to call me beautiful and how other guys always referred to me by my complexion. He said he was from Georgia, so dark-skinned women were everywhere. His upbringing allowed him to see past the physical and look at me at the level I had yearned for since I was little. He saw past the outside and looked at me from within.

When I was thirty-five, we dressed in our Sunday best and went to church; I usually sat towards the back. I wanted to be in the house, but I also wanted to blend in. One Sunday, I went up for extra prayer. Usually, when the preacher called the congregation up to the pulpit, I stood in my aisle near my seat and prayed with the surrounding people, but I felt a little down and wanted to feel closer to God that Sunday. I wanted to feel the spirit with the others at the front of the church who were hurting or needed encouragement.

I got up and moved to the front of the church for prayer. After prayer, we would hug those around us and walk back to our respective seats to prepare for the next part of service. As I walked back to my chair, greeting those around me, an older lady shook my hand. As she did, she looked at me and spoke. "How long did it take you to comprehend how beautiful you are?"

Her question shocked me, so I said, "Excuse me, ma'am?"

She repeated herself, then she said, "your skin is so pretty, but I bet you didn't realize it when you were younger. How long did it take you to comprehend how beautiful you are?"

I looked down at my hands holding her hands, then I said, looking up to meet her gaze.

"Not till recently, maybe within the past ten years."

"It's a shame it took you that long to see how beautiful you are," she said, then she let go of my hand and walked back to her seat.

I was in shock for the next week contemplating her question. "How long did it take me to realize I was beautiful?" Did I ever think I was beautiful? The more the question ran through my head, the more I realized I didn't think I was beautiful. Honestly, I didn't think I was anything. I cared about myself just enough to get by. Just enough to look somewhat put together, tidy, and conservative when I was out in public, a little sexy when out with friends or my husband. Nothing too flashy, too loud. Nothing to draw attention to. I'd made myself blend in and be labelless. Not cute, pretty, sexy, and damn sure, not beautiful. I was the color in a rainbow you didn't see from afar. I was there, you could see me, but I wasn't worth commenting on.

That lady helped me see that in someone's eyes, I was beautiful. I was worth it. Not just to my husband. He loved me because he chose me, but someone who didn't have a connection to me could see me as beautiful. From that day, I worked on learning to love my looks. I would put on more eye makeup, find a lipstick that I liked, and dress in colors I once hated, like yellow and green. I would try things and see If I liked them and not care what other people thought. Even now, though I don't make many bold decisions all at once, I'm learning how to feel beautiful, in my way, something I'd ignored for too long.

PERSPECTIVE:

I stopped looking in the mirror from the ages of eighteen till twenty-five. I looked at myself when I brushed my teeth and combed my hair to make sure it was in regulation, and I didn't have boogers hanging out of my nose, but I stopped "looking" at myself. I didn't groom in the mirror like other girls; along the way, I'd given up trying to change my appearance to "impress." Why? What was the point of looking different when I couldn't adjust the one thing I wanted to change? The something that made me feel least attractive and worthless was my skin tone. It was dark. I was born with this complexion, and nothing would change that. I ingrained in me that my self-worth was tied to my skin color. While I didn't go to the extremes of self-hate, like using face cream or hating other black people, avoidance became my coping mechanism. I'd avoid groups, but not just any groups—specifically sizeable crowds of Black people. I wasn't afraid of them physically hurting me; I was fearful of the emotional hurt: the bullying, the taunting, the teasing.

After I left high school, most of my female friends were White. I became the token; I hid behind them as if their whiteness protected me somehow, not from racism, but the reality of my skin tone. None of them ever commented on how dark I was or the texture of my hair. None of my White friends cared what I wore or how much my shoes cost. While I am sure they thought they gained some cool points or used their proximity to validate their acceptance of African Americans, I used them to validate my existence. My ability to make and keep friends and show I was more than just a skin color, that I had personality and value, that I could be funny and like other things and not feel like I was lame.

This mutual leeching served me well and prevented my complete self-destruction in a small way.

The close friends of other races I've gained and maintained, I've valued just as much, if not more, than my African American friends. They love me as a person, and I appreciate them for the individuals they are. They are the ones you want by your side in a fight, the ones I'd trust with my kids, and they'd do the same for me. They've allowed me to value all races and have shown my kids and me it doesn't matter what you look like on the outside; what matters is how people are supposed to treat and stand up for one another. During a time when I felt my race betrayed me, my friends of other races filled in the gaps and made me whole.

The harassment, for all its grief, allowed me to develop my empathic abilities like a superpower. I'm able to feel others' emotions, and I can pick up on people's intentions like a magnet. I can tell just by meeting someone if their intentions are pure and if they're someone, I want around my family. I like to share my empathetic instances with my husband. When I've met someone new, I attempt to describe how I feel on the inside and the conversation sounds like this.

"I met Master Sergeant Weaver today," I'd tell him while taking off my uniform.

"Really, where does he work? What's his job?" He'd ask while also changing out of his uniform into something more comfortable.

Then I'd detail who Master Sergeant Weaver was and where he works. Then I'd say, "I don't get a good vibe from him."

"Hmm, why not?" My husband asked.

"I'm not sure. I can't quite put my finger on it, but something's not quite right about him," I'd say and then leave it at that.

Weeks or months would go by, and then out of the blue, someone would tell me a story about Master Sergeant Weaver, or I'd mention his name in conversation. Then like clockwork, the person I'm speaking to would share their negative experience with Master Sergeant Weaver. Feelings of relief would wash over me as I discovered that my intuition was correct. When the gates opened, man, did they open up; it was then that I thanked God in my head for allowing me to pick up on that person's negative vibe and not let them into my life or near my family.

My empathic abilities led me to some of the most incredible friendships and conversations I've ever had in my life. They make me appreciative of the negative experiences of my past. It's allowed me to make meaningful, lasting connections as an adult. If any teenagers are reading this chapter, hang in there, keep seeking meaningful friendships, and they will come.

TOOLS THAT HELPED ME

The change came from finding the beauty within, practicing looking at myself in the mirror, and positive self-reflection. Instead of avoiding the mirror because I didn't want to see my dark skin, I started looking in the mirror, looking for a positive reflection. I forced myself to stare at my face and find at least one good thing I liked about myself.

"Well, I like my smile," I said to myself.

"And… I like my eyes."

Once I found those two things, my mirror journey looked slightly different. Every morning, I woke up and said to myself, "your eyes are amazing today." "Your smile is amazing today," I told those two things to myself every day, and eventually, I loved those parts of myself. Once I mastered those parts, I found other things I loved about myself and focused on those. Little by little, I discovered I liked myself, and once that happened, I could see the good in others.

People and groups I avoided because of past hurt as a child, I slowly immersed myself in them and embraced them. Did practicing positive self-reflection fix me immediately? No, but it allowed me to take positive steps toward finding love and genuine, lasting friendships. Am I still nervous before I step into new situations where I'm uncomfortable? Yes, but I've learned that if I don't step out there, I won't grow. I've also learned to listen to my inner voice. If you can master the ability to listen to your inner voice and trust yourself, it will give you the confidence to use self-love techniques and put yourself into the world.

Chapter 10

OUT FRONT

"I'd rather see your honest pain than a brave front." —Francine Rivers

Recently I discovered I didn't enjoy being out front. My cousin turned an old VHS tape of a family reunion from around 1990 into a DVD.

She gave me a copy, and I watched my family on tape. As I watched the video, the camera moved around a large park, capturing everyone on the video. As it moved past me, I watched the videographer say, "Say hi to the camera, Yonne."

I waved and skipped out of the frame. Then a few minutes later, I appeared on the camera again. But I did what I could to not be on the video. I've never been a fan of seeing myself on camera or in pictures. I don't even like to playback my voice mail messages out of fear of hearing my voice. It's funny, but I remember the moments that caused me to want to blend into the background.

When I was little, my mom gave me a pair of hand-me-down tap shoes. They were likely from my cousin Grace. She was only older than me by a couple of months, but she was at least four inches taller and a little bigger, so I received all her old clothes when she outgrew them. One year there was a pair of her old tap shoes, and my mom decided she would teach me to tap dance since we couldn't afford lessons.

"Look, Yonne, tap shoes," she said excitedly as we went through the black garbage bag of clothes. She had me put them on and taught me some of the first things you learn in dance class.

"I used to go to dance class every week, and we'd learn Tap and Jazz just like Alvin Ailey's dance school in New York." Then she'd shuffle around with a broad smile on her face.

From that day on, she made me tap in the hallway of our apartment on Lawndale Street in Chicago. "Shuffle ball chain step. Shuffle ball chain step, "she'd say to me as I danced up and down the hall on the tile floor.

"Shuffle ball step. Shuffle ball chain." I repeated her motions as the tap-tap sounds came from the shoes. Over and over, I'd practice from the front door to the back door. Then, she told me I looked like Shirley Temple as I got better. (I had a Jeri Curl) and my mom would sing. "On the good ship, lollypop. Sing Yonne!" she'd say. "Sing loud. Don't forget to smile."

She'd make me sing and practice that routine till my feet began to hurt. Then when her friends came over, I'd have to perform for them.

"Yonne! Come and say hi to so and so."

"Hi," I said, giving a shy wave and a toothless grin. Then my mother would say,

"She's learning how to tap dance. Doesn't she look like Shirley Temple?"

Most of this wasn't an issue until 1:00 a.m., and she was raging. She'd shake me awake to put on tap shoes to sing and dance for her high friends. I sang and danced for months, till my feet grew out of the shoes, and we had to give them away to another family.

As far back as I can remember, I've been writing. In 1992, I was twelve years old, and Tupac was the hottest rapper on the streets. We had a channel called "The Box," a music video order service, where you could call in and pay $1.99 and request a music video that "The Box" would play on the TV. I had no money to buy videos. Still, it was fun to watch the different music videos scroll across the screen. It was there that I saw the music video for "Brenda's Got a Baby."

I was hooked; it amazed me that girls were off somewhere getting pregnant at twelve, and then Brenda ended up dead. The video evoked such powerful emotions inside me, I was inspired to draft my own poems. The first one was called "Little Girl." about a teenager finding out she was pregnant and not knowing what to do. It ended with, "But what are you supposed to do? You're just a little girl."

I poured my heart into that poem and was proud of my words. I'd written it in my diary; it had a lock and key, and it was a private space for my thoughts. That is until my mom found it, she was in my room, looking for loose change so she could go score, picked the lock on my diary, and read my poem. As usual, If I was around, and she was raging. I became the focus I walked into the kitchen after school one day; my mom was sitting at the kitchen table with my grandmother sitting across from her. My eyes looked down at the table, and my heart raced.

"Aww, look at this cute little poem Yonne wrote," my mom said. "You're not having sex, are you?" she asked me. She jumped up out of the chair and came in my face. "You better not be having sex!" She shouted, "All it takes is one time, and you'll get pregnant!" she said, wagging her finger in my face. "Plus, sex hurts!"

She ripped the poem out of my diary and showed it to anyone that came by the house. Sometimes, she even made me read it out loud. I hated that poem. I hated everything about it. Every word that was once precious to be turned into a mockery.

From then on, I stopped writing unless it was an assignment or for the school newspaper. I refused to put words down on paper. I didn't want to be embarrassed during one of her rages again.

As I got older, I did trivial things to stand out. In my freshman year of high school, I joined the drama club and landed the lead in Romeo and Juliet. Surprisingly, my mother showed up for that performance and cheered loudly when the play was over.

I was on the gymnastics team. Gymnastics came easy to me. I learned how to flip, do cartwheels and balance myself from watching the Olympics. I didn't even need to audition, the coaches agreed to teach me what I didn't know. I learned how to pour myself into something. I found my focus. It was a team sport, but it was only me when I performed. If I made a mistake, I kept working on it.

We even had gymnastics meets against other high schools, and although our team never won first place, I snagged a few medals in balance beam and vault. My extended family showed up to watch me compete. But I was only on the team for two years before the school board cut girls' sports funding. After my short gymnastics career, I hung out in the background again, working on the school paper. I enjoyed the editing and cut-and-paste aspect of the entire process. I started writing again, but it was only a small book of poetry published by the school. I was proud of my work and found my writing spark.

I spent my junior and senior years in Naval Junior Reserve Officer Training School or NJROTC. Taking the class meant I didn't have to take gym class anymore, and it was something to do. I even worked my way up to the rank of ensign, and some of the kids looked up to me.

When winter formals and prom came around, I wanted to attend but didn't want to be fussed over or made up. I felt like there were too many eyes on me, too many people wanting to make me look like their image of what they thought I should be. I never thought my insides matched my outsides. I felt like either a fraud or looked like my mother.

Once I left home for the Air Force, it was easy to blend in; if I followed the rules and didn't make too much fuss, people left me alone. I found my comfort zone, not being out in front but not being in the back of the pack, either. I was comfortable. Shortly after September 11th, another high-ranking person suggested I work for the area commander in the Readiness Center. In that center, I would brief the officers on the events of the previous evening every morning. When I started the job, I worked the night shift after watching the process for a few months. One night, my trainer said. "Okay, you've seen enough. You're going to brief in the morning."

I worked all night on my report preparing for the early morning briefing. The first time I spoke, I was shaking in my boots. After I briefed the first time, the Commander started requesting that I report every day. He said he liked my voice. I could easily pronounce all the complex words, names, and countries. I'd finally found a use for my "white girl" voice. During that time, I was the lowest-ranking briefer. I enjoyed my job. Along the way, I learned I could speak intelligently about anything if I read the material once. I found my confidence, and if I remembered to slow down, I could talk in front of people with ease. After a while, I craved more individualized activities.

Participating in exercises like weightlifting and running marathons helped me increase my external confidence. I didn't need anyone to validate my performance, and I couldn't be a disappointment to anyone. I was responsible for my successes and failures. I'd broken away from my mother's shadow and into my light.

PERSPECTIVE

Some people need others around them all the time. I am fine doing things alone. I've learned to refine my gifts independently; I process most of my emotions alone, inside of my head. The problem with processing most of your feelings alone is, sometimes it sounds like noise. Over time, I've learned that I need others; having friends and family around to help you sort through the noise is beneficial, even though it was hard for me to share my gifts and talents with others. I had to share again and realize everyone wouldn't use my words against me. I now understand that sometimes we need to trust others just as we learn to trust ourselves.

As far as my career goes, I believe everything happens for a reason, and if something is meant for me, it will happen. While we do not know which direction life will take us, and we cannot change what happens to us, we can change how we react. I choose to take each thing as a lesson. What can I learn from what just occurred, and what can I do better if it happens again? I can choose to wallow in my failures and drown them with substances to numb the pain temporarily, or I can figure out what I need to learn from that experience and use it to push me further. I choose the latter since I've seen the path of the former.

TOOLS THAT HELPED ME

Finding my strengths. Gymnastics, running, and public speaking are personal accomplishments. No one else is in the light; no one else feels the success or failure. The focus is on me, and if I mess up, there is no one else to blame but me. No one else has control over my beam routine but me. If I fall off the beam, I lost my focus. If my run time during a race was slow, I didn't train hard enough. If I mispronounced a word, I didn't practice it enough. It has nothing to do with anyone else, and I carry the weight of success and failure on my back like a cross. I think that's why I enjoyed going back to school. I could gauge how much work I needed to put in to get the grade I wanted.

Stepping into my light meant I had to figure out my gifts and talents. Discovering my gifts allowed me to carve out a tiny piece of my place in the world; parts that were important to only me, things I could hang my hat on. While watching a TV show one night, I heard someone state that people do drugs, drink too much, or have addictions because they ignore their passions in life. The speaker then insinuated that if you ignore your genuine passion, the desire becomes so great that you use substances to numb the calling.

At the time, the statement sounded silly. I remember thinking, my mom is a drug addict because she's been ignoring her true calling in life. That's dumb.

But the more I thought about it, the more I think it's partially true after talking to people from all walks of life while in the military. I noticed a pattern; people feel the most at peace when using their gifts. When they aren't using their talents, or when family is pushing them in a direction they don't want to go, they spend lots of time thinking about their passions. It eats away at them like an itch they can't scratch, and substances become the answer.

I can't tell you how many hours I've spent dreaming of sitting up writing—the images in my head of penning miraculous novels, seeing my name in magazines and on bookshelves. I even imagined myself winning the Nobel prize for Literature.

I considered all the addicts worldwide, suppressing their gifts, and what could happen if they started embracing their passions instead. Along the way, someone told them no. Someone made them feel inadequate by dimming a light that needed to shine. One of the most important things you can do to get away from whatever shadow you think has been cast over you is to find the light inside you and fan those embers to ignite it. Doing so might change your life.

Chapter 11

CALCULATED STEPS

"There is no one giant step that does it, it's a lot of little steps."
— Peter A. Cohen

I can pinpoint the moments in my life that led me to determine that it was time to come up from under my mother's shadow and move into my light. Like pictures in a photo album, something ingrained in my memory became the positive building blocks of my life. When I finished peeling back the parts of me that worked so hard not to become my mother, there wasn't much left.

I'd put myself on birth control at sixteen. Okay, let's back up a bit. I lost my virginity at sixteen. The only reason I had sex at that age was that when I started my period at thirteen, my mother told me sex hurt and that I would instantly get pregnant if I did it.

"Yonne, please wait until you are at least sixteen." She'd speak.

So, like an excellent little teenager, I waited while listening to my mother ask me if I was having sex. She did this once every six months for the next three years. I couldn't wear a coat in the house, or baggy clothes, because she thought I was hiding something. Sometimes my mother would barge into the bathroom when I was getting out of the shower and ask me to drop my towel so she could see my stomach to check if it was growing. There was nothing there, and I had a flat stomach from all 200+ crunches each day for gymnastics practice.

Then, when the year I was to turn sixteen approached, I put my plan into motion. I didn't have a boyfriend and didn't want to be "that girl." The one who has a boyfriend falls in love, loses her virginity to them, and ends up pregnant and forced to get married to someone who didn't love her. That would not be my story. I'd write my own damn story and control the narrative so that I wouldn't get played. My first time having sex would be on my terms, with whom I chose.

I had a lot of male friends. We all hung out, drank, smoked cigarettes, and chilled after school. So, I decided I needed to pick one, let him know what I wanted and when, and make this thing happen. His name was Gregory, and he was a year older than me, but he spent a lot of time with us. He didn't have a girlfriend and didn't want one. He was doing his own thing. I simply had to work up enough nerve to ask him.

One day, we were at the park hanging out, and I was on a swing. He was walking past, so I called to him. "Hey Greg, come here."

"Okay." He walked over to the swing next to me. "What's up?"

Breathe, Yonne. You can do this. Control the situation. I told myself as I took a deep breath.

"So, my birthday is coming up in weeks," I started.

"Yeah," he said, "that's cool. How old are you going to be?"

"Sixteen," I said, glancing at the rocks below my feet.

"Oh, so you are having a party you want me to come to?" he said with a chuckle.

"Uh, no. I rolled my eyes, "I'm not having a party like that."

"Well, I'll just have to give you a gift," he said flirtatiously, winking at me.

" I need a favor," I said. I looked up across the park as I heard a bus pull up to the corner; I needed to make this quick before the rest of our friends got off the bus and reached us on the swings.

"What?" he asked, "Need me to get you a couple of bottles or something?"

"No, I want you to take my virginity," I mumbled," looking at my feet.

"Huh?" His eyes grew wide as he ran his hand over the side of his head.

I grew more confident with my words as I repeated my request.

"I know we don't go together or anything, but I want this to happen, and I trust that if we do it, you won't go telling all my business." When he didn't answer right away, I added, "Look, I don't need a yes or no right now. You have a couple of weeks to let me know."

Then I got up off the swing and walked away, leaving him sitting on the swing, stunned at my question. I headed towards the corner where the bus stop was to meet my friends to ride home. I felt bold and more in charge of my life than before. Now, if I didn't get pregnant, everything would work out.

One day, as it drew closer to my birthday, Gregory slid into the empty seat next to me on the bus on the way home. My girlfriends were sitting on the other side of me, talking.

Greg leaned closer to me despite the loud bus banter and said lowly. "Okay."

I looked him in the eye. "Okay, what?"

"Okay, we can have sex," he said with a grin.

"Look, I don't want you to do anything you don't want to do. I'm not looking for you to be my boyfriend or anything. This can be a onetime thing, and I won't get attached to you."

"I know," he said, "I'm good with it. How do you want to do this?"

"Well, we can't do it at my house. I have people there all day," I said.

"Okay, we can do it at my house. My mom will be at work on Saturday. You can come over then. About 2:00."

"Okay, Saturday at 2:00."

I looked up and realized the bus was at my stop. "All right, bye," I said as I hopped up and slung my backpack on my shoulder.

As I got off the bus, I felt butterflies in my stomach. This was happening. I was in control.

As the day grew closer, I became more nervous. Would I get pregnant? What if I caught a sexually transmitted disease? What if people in the school found out? In all the uncertainty, I knew one thing for sure. I needed to get on birth control if I would have sex regularly. I wouldn't be like my mother.

That first experience was an experiment. It wasn't magical, nor horrible. I'd give it a seven if I had to rate first times based on my limited experience. I liked it enough to do it again. Greg and I messed around all summer. Then when school started, he got a girlfriend, which I was okay with because we were not a couple. Just what the kids say, "friends with benefits." Shortly after my first experience, I started my research on how to get birth control.

My grandmother planted the idea to join the service in my brain. My school started a Navy Junior Reserve Office Course (NJROTC) during my junior year of high school. After the school canceled the gymnastics program because of funding, I wasn't trying to go back to regular gym class. So, when I found out I could take NJROTC instead of gym, I jumped at the opportunity. I enjoyed NJROTC, a different type of class, and an easy A. All I had to do was memorize some Navy terms, wear a uniform once a week, and carry a fake gun.

Plus, my best girlfriends were in the class, which gave us a chance to get together during the day. NJROTC set me apart from the rest of the kids and gave me a little responsibility. No one talked about me. There was structure, and it wasn't a popularity contest. This class was about ability. If you could do something, you excelled. You'd hang out in the background and blend in if you couldn't.

A quarter way through my junior year, the possibility of the military as a life choice came into play. They offered the Armed Services Aptitude Test (ASVAB) during one of our class periods. My friends and I decided to take the test to get out of class. Little did we know that one choice would lead to much more. I found it relatively easy when I took the test, and I was done quickly. My score was high enough to get into all the services. Since the score was good for two years, I wouldn't even have to retake the test my senior year.

When I showed it to my grandmother, she suggested I consider going into the military. She'd heard that they would pay for my education and healthcare, and I'd see the world while earning a paycheck. It was a win-win for everyone. I wasn't sure about leaving home since all I knew was Chicago and California. As I continued going to NJROTC, I thought about joining the Navy; since I was completing some of the courses in high school, I could enter the Navy or the Coast Guard at a higher rank. I knew nothing about the other services. When I talked to my family about it, some said, "Go to college, don't go into the service." They thought I'd get sent to war and die. All of that swirled through my mind as I got closer to my senior year and made my decision. My grandmother suggested I join the Air Force or the Navy since you never hear about Navy or Air Force people dying in a war.

The turning point came after receiving a phone call from the Air Force recruiter.

"Who are you talking to?" She asked,

The question alone would send any teenager to their room, not me. I was on the cusp of building a future for myself that didn't include my mother.

"I'm on the phone, Mom." I rolled my eyes, which didn't go well, and she got louder.

"Who are you talking to, Yonne," she yelled and moved closer.

"I'm on the phone," I yelled back. "I'm sorry, sir, I'll have to talk to you another time," I said to the Air Force recruiter, then I hung the phone up on the wall and walked over to the sink.

"That was rude. I was on the phone," I said to her.

"Who were you talking to?" she asked again.

The warning in her tone should have been enough to make me tell her what she wanted to know. For years I had been on the receiving end of her tirades, and for once in my life, I had the potential to go anywhere and be anything other than her daughter.

"I was talking to the Air Force recruiter. I took the ASVAB test at school, and my scores were good enough to enlist in the Air Force," I said.

"You're not going into the Air Force!" my mom insisted.

"I might. I'll be eighteen. You won't be able to tell what to do anymore."

"You don't even want to go into the military. Your grandmother wants you to go."

"How do you know? I might want to go." I said before moving to the sink to wash the dishes. The heat of the water bit into my hands, and for once, I was grateful. At least she couldn't see what her questions were doing to me.

She turned and yelled at me. "Why! Why do you want to join the Air Force?"

I looked at her and squinted my eyes; I could feel the anger rising inside of me. And without a second thought, I said, "I want to go, so I don't end up like you!" Rolling my neck in a circle and smacking my lips.

In slow motion, I watched my mother pull her hand back and slap me across my face. It felt like I was watching a movie until the sting snapped me back to reality. I gasped as the tears welled in my eyes; I left the kitchen and ran up to my room. As I lay on my bed sobbing, I knew I had to move away when I graduated, be it college or the military. I had to get away from my mother.

We never spoke about that conversation again; I went to see the recruiter with my grandmother for the first time. Then I went back a few months later with my mother and grandmother. Even though I spoke to the recruiter, I still took my college entrance exams, applied to three colleges, and prayed I could get accepted. In my senior year, I was accepted to two of the three schools I applied to and still had the military waiting in the wings. All I had to do was not get arrested, avoid becoming pregnant, and graduate. All three I could do easily.

With the three options in front of me, I had to decide my fate. Go to college, figure out how to pay for it, or join the military and remove me from everything I'd ever known. Everyone in my family had opinions of what I should do, but no one was coughing up any money to make college a reality. Honestly, I was tired of school. I didn't know what I wanted to be when I grew up, but I didn't want to spend four years working toward a degree, only to wake up three years in and realize that I wanted to change my major. I needed to get away from Nire and figure out what I wanted to do with my life; I felt like I was suffocating, and I needed air. So, I joined the military.

Once I made that decision. The question now became, which branch do I join? Do I go into the Navy and spend my time on a boat? Or do I join the Air Force and keep my feet on the ground? I always say things happen for a reason, and my decision, be it life-changing, was a shallow one. While I was in NJROTC, they promoted me to ensign, making me an officer for the upcoming school year. This promotion required me to attend a leadership camp for a week during spring break. This camp was in Great Lakes, IL, where the Naval boot camp was located. I spent a week eating at the chow hall, living in the barracks, and learning the Navy way.

We had to take showers in open bays during the camp, with zero privacy, just like the people in boot camp. When it was my turn to take a shower, I went in and turned on the water. Since I was in the first group to shower, the water hadn't run all day. Giant water bugs came out of the drains when I turned on the faucet. I was so disgusted and decided that I was joining the Air Force right then and there.

PERSPECTIVE

What's so ironic about that story is that not eighteen months later, after I graduated from Air Force Basic Training, I was up early waiting for a bus. I was scheduled to catch a flight to my first technical training and needed to wait near the bushes. As I was standing by the bushes, I looked down. What did I see crawling all over the bushes? Damn water bugs. Who knew a roach would decide my fate? That decision led to my journey towards finding my light, and this book. So, as I said, all things happen for a reason.

TOOLS THAT HELPED ME

Courage, to break away. I had to make the decision for my life on my own and go against everything I'd ever known. Even though I received advice from family and friends, the decision to join the military was up to me. Was it scary? Yes, but wise men say success lies outside your comfort zone and on the other side of fear. Not many people I grew up with dared to move away from Chicago. They were so afraid of what could go wrong they failed to ask themselves what could go right mustering up the courage to move away and make a life on my own set the stage for my journey and success. It's easy to stay in one spot afraid of what is outside of your hometown but having the courage to move to seek new experiences allows you to try new things, meet different people and expand your mind. There is a point in one's life where we cannot bloom where they are planted. One might have to pick up the pot and settle in new soil and new light to experience real growth.

Chapter 12

GETTING HELP

Be strong enough to stand alone, smart enough to know when you need help, and brave enough to ask for it. — Zaid K. Abdelnour

The first time I remember getting "help" in dealing with my "mommy" situation, I was eleven or twelve years old. My stepmother took my three sisters and me to a conference. She was a psychologist and a recovering addict herself. She decided we were old enough to attend the annual Alcoholic Anonymous Founder's Day Conference. My stepmom, two sisters, my niece, and I piled into the car and made the six-hour drive to Akron, Ohio.

In the car, she said, "You're going to attend the Al-Anon meetings."

I did not know what that was or why I needed to go, but it wasn't Chicago, and I wasn't around my mom, so I didn't argue.

In one weekend, I learned what an Al-Anon was, what an enabler was, and what I could do as a kid to deal with a parent who was on drugs. They told us it wasn't our fault, that abuse of a controlled substance is an illness and that our parents were sick, but they could only get better if they wanted to. Back then, I didn't know if I believed all the dogma they preached, but I discovered other kids out there like me; I wasn't alone.

Until that point, no one talked about what my mom did or explained that she was on drugs and how it affected me. My family didn't openly talk about her issues. It was like having a bull in a China shop run around and break all the items. The owners just cleaned up the broken pieces, put new china back on the shelf, and opened business the next day, hoping no one noticed. Even though the bull got put out of the shop every few days, it would come back. Everyone knew it was the bull, but nobody said anything to stop it from coming into the shop out of fear of upsetting the bull even more. Everyone just tried to pray the anger out of the bull.

That weekend let me know I wasn't crazy; it wasn't me. Sadly, I realized my actions would not make my mother stop doing drugs. She would have to hit rock bottom to climb back out, and my entire family and I were along for the ride.

I was twenty the second time I remember getting "help" with my mommy situation. I'd joined the Air Force and lived away from my mother. They stationed me in Maryland, and I was living my best life in my apartment. I needed to take a test to become proficient at my new job. It required me to study hard on my own time while learning the hands-on portion at work. I couldn't study during the workday, so I needed to study before or after working a twelve-hour shift. When I took the test, I scored 63%, and I needed 65% to pass. I was devastated and had frequent panic attacks. I tried to deal with the panic attacks on my own, but they got so bad I felt I couldn't leave my apartment—the attacks presented as fear, especially during harsh weather.

One day it was raining, I had an errand to run and while I was driving, the weather got worse, and I started to hyperventilate. If I didn't pull over, I would have an accident and, in my mind, die a horrific death. Eventually, I pulled myself together well enough to drive back home. I never got to where I was going; that's when I decided I needed to get help.

I went to see my first therapist and explained my experience in the car, and she asked me if anything significant had just happened. I told her about the course failure and that I feared being kicked out of the military and returning home. That fear consumed me. By working with the counselor, I distinguished that I somehow felt that my course failure would turn me into a crack head. She wanted to put me on anti-anxiety medication, but I refused. Instead, we had six months of intense weekly sessions. It was enough to clear my mind to realize what I could and couldn't control. I could understand that the failure of a course didn't equate to failing in life.

While attending therapy, I wanted to go home on vacation, but the thought of going back crippled me. I felt conflicted between visiting my family and friends but not wanting to see my mother. I told the therapist that my mother was like a tornado. They form out of nowhere, and when they spin, they destroy everything in their path on a random course—leaving some houses perfect and standing while leveling others to the ground. One day during my session, I told my therapist. "I feel like she sucks the air out of a room." Throughout my sessions, as I cried in the oversized chair, she taught me how to put on a "gas mask" to go home, visit my family, and make it out alive. I expressed my fears about my visit. We went over what to do if my mother asked me for money and how to make sure my possessions didn't get stolen. I made it through my visit and that obstacle in my life. I passed the test on my second attempt and remained in the Air Force. The first therapist taught me about boundaries. I learned why I needed them with my mother and how to get them from her and other people respectfully.

I thought I was "cured". I could put on my pretend gas mask and move forward with life. Being so busy with work, the home visits increased, but I was okay. When I called home, my grandmother told me my mother was improving and how she'd stopped doing drugs and joined the church and volunteered at my cousins' school. I didn't fully believe it since she'd done it before as good as it sounded. I became slightly jealous that she got her life together enough to do everything for my cousins that she never did for me.

PERSPECTIVE

PPeople preach about asking for help, but the sheer act of opening their mouths to vocalize that they aren't okay is hard. Before I made the phone call to my first therapist. I prayed… prayed as I struggled through the panic attacks. I prayed as I poured the drinks to hide my fears. When I felt prayer wasn't working, sleep and books became my two best friends. Dreaming of worlds I longed to be a part of instead of my current reality. Thinking I could sleep and wake up as one of the heroes in the tales I consumed, only to open my eyes the next day realizing everything was the same. None of it worked until I got the courage to go back to my first love, writing and type an email to the one person I trusted. Even when I couldn't find the words to say what was wrong, typing them out gave me the space and the time to request the help I needed.

TOOLS THAT HELPED ME

Reaching out. As simple as it sounds, it was the hardest thing to do. When your mind is spinning like a tornado, it's hard to focus on one thing that could stop the spinning. I felt like there wasn't anyone I could trust until I realized there was a trained psychologist in my tribe. My stepmother was a trained counselor and a keeper of other people's thoughts. If she could do that for others, surely, she could do the same for me. So, I sat down and sent her an email. I shared with her how I was feeling and what was going on in my life, and she emailed me back. She responded without judgment or shame; she understood what I was going through and offered suggestions to help me. She also made me promise I'd see someone in person. She offered me a life raft and gave me the courage I needed to call a therapist and start my journey towards getting the help I needed.

Chapter 13

GRIEF

"Grieving doesn't make you imperfect it makes you human." — Sara Dessen

Grief is a funny thing. Sometimes it becomes a supernova right in front of your face, blocking out everything and everyone. Other times, it masquerades as anger or fear. And then there is the numbness, like after a long, violent storm. The pieces of your life litter the street, and you wonder if you need them anymore.

Saying goodbye only hurts when the person meant something to you, good or bad. You think about the missed opportunities and remnants of a relationship deferred. When a family member or a friend has an addiction, it bleeds into every aspect of your life. It colors everything, from your choice in heading off to college to seeing the world.

A year later, I moved to Japan and embraced the culture and its people a million miles away from the life I once knew. I began college and even enjoyed speaking to my mother in short phone conversations. While I was in Japan, I needed to come back to the States for a class in Florida. While I was there, I went to see my mother; she'd suffered a stroke about nine months earlier from excessive drinking, smoking, and drug use. The doctor told her that she would die if she smoked another cigarette or had another drink. According to my grandmother, I guess that was her wake-up call because she stopped everything cold turkey. I'd made plans for her to come to my graduation from my course so she could see how well I was doing. She attended the commencement and spent the weekend with me before I flew back to Japan. We had a good time. I remember talking to God about how this visit was different and hoped we could rebuild our relationship.

Two weeks after I flew back to Japan, my mother suddenly died in her sleep. It's weird because the last time I saw her was on April 6th. Her Birthday was April 11th, and she died on April 28th. I took this hard, so hard that I flipped out at her funeral. I held it together until the last part of the ceremony, where everyone walked past the open casket to pay their last respects. When they opened the coffin and folded down the blanket, she looked asleep.

"Somebody wake her up! You know how she's always the last one to wake up!" I yelled.

"Wake my momma up and tell her it's time to go!" I shouted; my brother held me up as we went past the casket. I must have blacked out because the next thing I remember, I'm in the limo with my brother. He was trying to get me to drink some water and cleaning my face with some tissue. Suddenly there was a tapping on the limousine door. As my brother rolled the window down, a lady was rocking back and forth. In a slurred tone, she said,

"Hey, baby, you, okay? Damn, you look just like yo momma!"

My brother rolled the window up, and I said, "Who was that?"

My brother replied, "Hell, I don't know." We both started laughing; my tears of sorrow turned to tears of joy.

The next couple of weeks were a blur as I spent some time with my family. Helped my grandmother go through my mother's things from her room and flew back to Japan. When I returned to my room on the base, I began to unpack when I noticed a Mother's Day card on the dresser. I purchased it for my mother weeks earlier. I used to buy her Mother's Day cards, but I chose the most generic message I could find when I picked them out. I hoped she would get the hint that our relationship wasn't Hallmark-worthy one day.

But there the card sat on the dresser, no address and now no mother to give it to.

As I processed my grief, I started to blame myself, thinking I made my mom die because I prayed for her to "go away" when things were bad. I repeatedly prayed for God to take her away from my grandmother so she'd have money, and her items wouldn't get stolen anymore. She wouldn't have died if I hadn't asked God to make her go away. I sat with this altered reality in my heart for years, bearing a false burden that wasn't mine to carry.

All the miles that I traveled and the places and people that became a part of my world, the unfinished business of my relationship with my mother always felt like a boomerang. No matter how far away life carried me, everything circled back to my mother.

Perspective

Eventually, I realized I didn't "make my mother go away". After years of drinking, drugs, and smoking, her arteries hardened. And her heart and brain couldn't take the damage anymore and gave out. She made herself go away, and nothing I could've done or not done would ever change that. I also realized how much control I have over my own life. Going to therapy helped me lay the path I needed to progress from a girl to a young woman. Therapy also helped me understand how our inner child affects our outer adult. Practicing how to identify how I respond to situations, and if the response is coming from my inner child or my outer adult, keeps me in check and helps me avoid a lot of drama.

Tools that helped me

Break out your violin and your Cable TV love story. The Tools That Helped Me were time and boundaries. There's no way to predict when memories or flashbacks occur or when a buried trigger will hit you like a land mine. It's scary and can cause you to fold into yourself and avoid your life. But the more time you take to uncover the experiences that planted the land mines, the better you can get at identifying the warning sign of the triggers as you approach them. Time doesn't heal all wounds, but time allows scabs to cover the sting.

Learn how to set boundaries. I can't stress this enough, get clear about what you need. To step into your light and stay there, you must figure out your rules, what you will and will not tolerate, and stick to them. Otherwise, you'll go back and forth between what you need and what everyone else needs. Sometimes it's challenging to set boundaries because we don't know-how, and we are taught that we don't draw the line with family. This couldn't be farther from the truth. If you don't set your boundaries, you can't tell if you're being emotionally hijacked into doing things that you don't want to do, taking you away from the path into your light.

Take some time and ask yourself a couple of questions. What do you need to feel safe, stable, and happy? Who is in the way of you achieving those feelings of safety, stability, and happiness? Once you answer those two questions, you've just identified your boundaries and who you need to set boundaries with. Once that's complete, you put on your oxygen mask and prepare for turbulence because those you need to set boundaries with won't be happy. They're used to pushing and pulling you emotionally into their mess and their needs causing you to lose sight of what you need and your light.

If you need help to express your feelings, then write them down. Prepare a script of what you need to say to set the boundary. After you've shared what you need to say to the offender, stick to your boundaries and start working towards achieving feelings of safety, stability, and happiness. Maybe you need a new job, or to go out of state for school, or in my case, it involved me joining the military. While I don't suggest taking extreme measures, it might become necessary to move into your light.

Chapter 14

The Awakening

If I could just wake up in a different place, at a different time, could I wake up as a different person? — Chuck Palahniuk

My first awakening came on my 34th birthday. I planned to jump out of an airplane and spend time with my friend Jasmine. She came into town, and we planned to go up to Austin to pick up her friend's daughter Danielle and stop at the outlet mall on the way back down to San Antonio. All went well until we were on our way home. We went to the outlet mall, had some retail therapy, and headed back to San Antonio. Shortly after we entered the city, her son, who was strapped in the car's back seat, looked up from his tablet and said,

"Mommy, I need to go to the bathroom."

"Okay, baby, we're almost home. Can you try to hold it till we get there?"

"Okay," Darnell said.

We drove past a few more exits before he said again,

"Mommy, I have to go to the bathroom bad."

I told Jasmine to get off at the next exit because I thought there was a McDonalds where he could use the restroom. Jasmine turned on her blinkers to get off at the next exit. As she reached the exit, she didn't notice the speed limit dropped from 65 mph on the expressway down to 15 mph as we made a 90-degree turn. Jasmine drove around the curve, and the car was still going at least 45 mph. Before we knew it, the SUV went up on two wheels and flipped on its side. It slowly tumbled over and landed upside down in a clearing on the side of the road. I screamed, Jasmine screamed, Danielle screamed, and Darnell started to cry.

"Oh shit! Oh shit," I yelled. All of us were suspended upside down and held up by the seatbelts. Jasmine yelled for her son, Darnell.

"Darnell, are you okay?"

All I heard was Darnell crying. I tried to look behind me since she couldn't see and noticed he was also suspended upside down, still strapped in his seat belt. Danielle was quiet.

I screamed, "Danielle! Are you all right?"

"Yes," Danielle said slowly as she checked over her body. "I think I'm okay. I'm just stuck."

"Okay, look, we have to get out of the car. Fluids are leaking, so we have to get out and away from the car."

Jasmine released her seat belt and fell to the roof of the car. She crawled out and grabbed Darnell from the car seat and moved him several feet away into an open grassy area.

I unbuckled my seatbelt and landed hard on my right shoulder. Then I helped Danielle out of her seat belt, and we scrambled toward the open area. When we got out and looked each other over, another car pulled up, and the passengers got out to see if we were okay. We were fine—just a couple of cuts from the glass, but nothing broken or life-threatening.

I hurried back to the vehicle, grabbed my purse and phone, and called my husband to tell him we were in an accident, and I needed him to come and pick me up. Jasmine called her friend Shonda and asked her to come and get her and the kids. Once the initial shock passed and the police department was on the way to the scene, Jasmine broke down. I went to her and held her; while she cried and said she was sorry. We started to go over what could've happened. How could we not notice the speed limit change? When the cops arrived, they explained we were not the first car crash at this very spot. They told us that many people miss the speed limit change. The police filed an accident report and offered to call an ambulance, but we refused since we weren't injured.

"Happy Birthday," Jasmine said to me.

"Damn, if you didn't want to be my friend anymore, you could've told me. You didn't have to roll the car," I said with a nervous chuckle.

We nervously laughed and hugged tighter than we'd ever hugged before. Both of us were grateful to be alive and unharmed and thankful the kids were okay. My husband showed up shortly after to take me home. He had our kids in the car. I ran to the car, flung open the doors, and kissed them. We waited for Shonda to arrive before we left the scene. I was quiet on the way home, mentally replaying what happened. I was just in a rollover car accident and survived. Later that night, after I ate and showered, I was in bed. My husband joined me, wrapped his arms around me, and rubbed my hair.

"You alright?" he asked.

"Yeah, I'm fine. You know that was one of my recurring nightmares."

"What?" he asked, pulling back to look at me.

"I used to have recurring nightmares about being in a rollover accident. But in my dreams, the car explodes, like in the movies, and I'm trapped inside." Tears started streaming down my face. "My dream was so scary, but the accident was nothing like my dream," I said.

"Dreams always show us the worst-case scenario. But dreams don't account for airbags, seatbelts, or cars with crumple zones," he said, pulling me closer.

"Our nightmares never account for advancements in technology." Then he kissed me on my forehead.

"This is true. I'm glad it was nothing like my dreams," I said.

"Me, too," he agreed. Then he kissed me on my lips, squeezed me tighter, and held me until I fell asleep. I haven't dreamed of rollover car crashes since the accident. The rollover crash with fireballs was a thing from the movies. My nightmares didn't hold a candle to the truth.

A couple of days after the accident, I jumped out of that airplane. Even though it was a tandem jump, it was one of the most freeing experiences. As I rode back from my adventure, I passed the spot where we had had the accident a couple of days earlier. My chest got tight, and I felt scared again, but I took a couple of deep breaths. As I reflected on what I'd gone through, I asked God why I got into an accident, so like my nightmares? God, what are you trying to tell me? Then the answer came to me just as clear as day. When are you going to write the book? This isn't the first time I've put this on your heart. So, when are you going to follow through? I sighed. "Okay, God," I said to myself. I'm going to do it. I'll write the book; I don't need another sign.

PERSPECTIVE

My friend Cori and I share a joke about being hard-headed believers. We don't see or hear God's signs the first time around, and people say. "If you don't do what God says when he whispers, you'll damn sure do it when he yells." That car accident was God screaming at me and telling me what I was supposed to be doing with my life. I'd ignored the whispers pulling on my heart for long enough. It was time to shut up and color.

For years, I've wanted to write a book about my life. God placed it on my heart when I was a teenager, and like most people, I ignored it—moving in other directions, avoiding sharing my story. From the time of the accident till I put letters to a Word document took another seven years. But I promised God, I'd write it. Against fear, doubt, and hesitation, I made it happen. Looking back, I think just about everything else I'd done up to this point was a distraction.

When I started searching for my purpose back in 2013, until I started drafting this book in 2019, other things I tried never made sense or felt right going to school, studying for promotion, moving my way up through military ranks were all work. This moment right now doesn't feel like work. It feels like freedom, like a symphony. It feels like home.

TOOLS THAT HELPED ME

Finding my why, I'd put off writing my book for so long because of fear, fear of what others would think, fear of rejection, fear of the praise I might receive, and fear of what people would think about me. I'd been the target of scrutiny and ridicule for so long that I'd put myself under the same microscope I'd avoided. It wasn't until I found my why that the words started to flow. My why gave me courage, my why gave me hope, my why became my push. If there's something that you've avoided doing, maybe start with asking yourself why you want to do it. You might be surprised to discover your why is bigger than your fear, and you can begin to use your why to push yourself out of your shadow.

Chapter 15

BREAKTHROUGH

"For things to reveal themselves to us, we need to be ready to abandon our views about them." — Thich Nhat Hanh

Over the years since then, I've managed my emotions well. The first year after my mother's death was challenging. My son was born three years later, and I'd imagine what she would say or do if she were around. I wouldn't make promises to my kids I couldn't keep. They may have disappointments in life, but I wouldn't be one of them. My kids would be proud of me, who I am, and what I've become.

I went years between therapy appointments and felt okay until 2018. After a challenging year at work, I woke up the morning after Columbus Day, feeling like the walls were crashing around me and angry about my career. After months of setbacks and professional disappointments, I felt lost. I decided to give therapy one more try, but this time do the work. I walked into the therapist's office, and the first words out of my mouth were, "Why am I here?"

I had to clarify because my therapist thought I was suicidal for the first fifteen minutes. I told her that I didn't intend on harming myself or others, but I needed to know why I still put the uniform on. Why was I trying when what I poured into others wasn't reciprocated in the way I felt like it needed to be?

So, after months in therapy, I decided it was time to hang up my uniform, but we discussed why I didn't want to. What did I have waiting for me on the other side? We discussed why I felt like I could not stand on my own. We tore into the areas where I felt weak, trying to make them stronger so that I could stand on my own when I retired. The breakthroughs came in spurts. Instead of saying I couldn't do something, I asked why not me? If other people could reach their goals, put out a book on Amazon, start blogs, and become full-time writers, why not me? What was so wrong with me that I couldn't do it too? Or what was so right with them that allowed them to stand in their light?

What brought me to counseling was a feeling of uncertainty. I had been throwing out stones and hopping from one to the other for so long, and now I'd run out of stones to throw, so I had nothing to jump to. I felt stuck, angry, and anxious. While I'm still nervous about things, I'm not as mad as before. I gained confidence in my ability to handle what happens to me and make the best of my time in my current situation— knowing that it is temporary and that a change will come.

I dove deep into many self-help books to understand the inner voice lying to me. That was who I was fighting. Other people weren't the battle; it was against myself and my mental limitations. I began to understand that I needed to change my mind set to reach my goals. So, I started to write down my dreams. This is not the first time I've ever written about my dreams or my why's, but this was the first time I felt it. I'd written the five affirmations below at the beginning of the year:

I deserve to get to my pre-baby weight.

I deserve to have my book published.

It's okay to pay off my debts and have money.

I deserve to live the life of my dreams.

I deserve to be a published author.

And while the affirmations above were all fine and dandy, they weren't deep enough; I needed to dig deeper. I'd gotten into saying my affirmations on my way home from the gym in the mornings. Every day I'd recite the same crappy ones above, and that's when the language changed.

I deserve to get to my pre-baby weight.

I deserve to have my book published.

It's okay to pay off my debts and have money.

I deserve to live the life of my dreams.

I am worthy of being a published author.

After saying the above, I changed the words.

I am worthy of being an author.

I am good enough to become an author.

I am good enough to have my words help others.

I am good enough to live the life of my dreams.

And that's when it all clicked. I am good enough, and I am worthy. I'd somehow convinced myself that I wasn't good enough all this time. In my past, I wasn't good or powerful enough to stop the bad things that happened to me from occurring because I wasn't good enough. I wasn't good enough to make my mother stop doing drugs and to love me drug-free. I wasn't good enough to get the kids that bullied me in school to stop picking on me. So how could I help anyone do anything of value? I felt unworthy; I felt worthless.

And that, ladies and gents, is when the tears fell. I felt inadequate even though I'd done all the things black women should do to be successful. Get married, have kids, get your degree, and land a good job. There it was, lying under the surface. Ms. Inadequacy. The mask I felt I'd been wearing made me appear to have it all together. The advice I'm able to give others, I cannot take myself. Ms. Worthlessness, the fear of not being able to stand on my own, and any slight misstep would send me spiraling into my mother's life. Ms. Useless, I'd always said the Devil attacked my self-worth. When I thought I'd figured things out, those feelings of "What in the hell do you think you're doing? You can't do this." Come back.

The internal message plays like a loudspeaker. —You aren't good enough, so why reach for the stars when you couldn't change your mother. You couldn't change the kids that picked on you, so how could you possibly be successful doing what you love when you couldn't even get the things you wanted the most in all the world to work out in your favor?

As I made the connections in my brain, tears streamed down my face. I said my new affirmation louder in the car.

I am worthy of having others read my books.

I am worthy of being debt-free.

If I get money, my mother will not take it away.

I deserve to have the life of my dreams.

I am worthy.

It felt like a floodgate of emotions opened inside of me. I felt strong and weak at the same time. I felt scared, like when I was little, but it's different now because she's dead, so I felt silly. As if this tiny thought loop was what had been holding me back.

Have I really been feeling worthless? Is that the right word? The breakdown of the word means not to have value. It didn't work when I used my voice to make the kids stop picking on me. It didn't work. The actions I took to get my mother to stop taking the drugs didn't work, or I wasn't worth her stopping. So, since I wasn't valuable enough to stop her, yes, worthless is the right word.

I tell people some kids are killing themselves over the type of stuff said to me when I was growing up. I get it; I understand why the kids are killing themselves. They've let another person convince them they have no value. A bully uses their words to make others feel worthless, so they deem themselves unworthy. Kids of substance abuse users feel powerless because they can't make their parents stop using. If you loved me, you'd stop; you wouldn't drink anymore. If I meant anything to you, you'd give me the money. I'm your mother. Don't I mean anything to you?

The back-and-forth exchange of worth makes self-esteem seem transactional instead of automatic. Then children feel worthless and weak and succumb to the same fate as their parents. The transaction is passed from person to person, parent to child, and curses are passed from generation to generation.

PERSPECTIVE

What if someone told you the monsters never really go away? The reality is that what no one talks about is that the demons we faced as kids never go away. Maybe if more people talked about them, we could prepare. What if some upstanding adult came to us as kids and said,

"Hey, the things you went through as a kid will shape you and leave you bruised and scarred, then you'll grow up and do some semi-successful stuff but guess what? The monsters you thought you put away will never really go away."

The monsters get buried under other things. We cover them by being strong, and focus on our education, being the provider, and not depending on anyone. But no, everyone's walking around fighting solo battles with mental monsters. These things we went through as kids are not one-time battles that don't come back. We think that once we slay one monster, we will never see them again, but no. They come back, hiding in the corners, waiting for the perfect time when life is right, then they pop out. "Surprise!"

The monsters may not be as gigantic as before, but they're still there. Maybe if someone told us they'd come back, we could prepare ourselves to deal with them another day.

TOOLS THAT HELPED ME:

If you haven't figured it out by now, the one tool that helped me was going to therapy and doing the work. Get ready to clutch your pearls. Prayer and church are cool and all, but you need a licensed therapist to help you sort through whatever you've got going on in your head. Therapists are trained to give you tools to help you change your perspective and thought process.

They provide a perspective that you haven't considered and are trained to deal with, situations where you might need medical intervention. I've talked to faith-based psychologists that integrate the bible into sound, psychological practices. If you believe in a higher power, it's like getting two golden tickets for the price of one. The point is to try to handle things on your own, praying for it, or dumping your problems onto your friends might not be enough.

You need someone who doesn't know you personally to provide you with advice and call you out on your bullshit. The longer you wait to put in the work, the longer it will take you to step into your light. Life is too short not to pursue what will make you truly happy. I was able to find and step into my light because I was willing to ask for help and do the work. I was ready to relive the anxiety and difficulties of the past emotions I spent so much time repressing and ignoring. So, my friends, put in the work and find a good therapist.

Chapter 16

ACCOMPLISHMENT AND FINDING YOU

"It's not who you are that holds you back, it's who you think you're not."
— Denis Waitley

Well, what happens now? Have I stepped into my light? Have I avoided all my mother's pitfalls and what I perceived as failures in her life? Working to not repeat them on my own? Some would say yes, I've married a man who loves me to no end and have two kids that I'll do anything for. I've finished a successful twenty-two-year military career. I have degrees on the wall, and I'm a published author. On the outside, the answer is yes.

On the inside, I've gone back and forth with drinking at a young age and smoking eleven years on and off. I deal with bouts of anxiety and the internal battle of self-doubt every day. The things I deal with internally are the same pressures my mother dealt with.

And the boomerang circles once more and lands near my mother. Women fear and often dread becoming like their mothers. I know I did.

Negotiating with monsters that go away and reappear is never an easy thing. The difference, which doesn't make me better or worse, is how I've dealt with them. It's easy to let the rage, sadness, and worthlessness eat away at my resolve. Allowing the voices of doubt to convince me not to push forward is a familiar old song. If hard-pressed, I could probably tap dance to it or use them as an excuse to prevent new things from coming into my life.

I've been there.

You've been there. I get it, but here's the kicker. Just because we land there doesn't mean we have to stay there.

Embrace the monsters, figure out where they come from, and slay them. By doing so, you are empowered to feel strong and capable of doing anything that comes your way. The waves of adversity don't go away, but by embracing them when they arrive, you can ride them and live to tell the tale.

Much like the lesson in the movie Soul. When Joe, played by Jamie Foxx, stood outside the club after playing with Miho. Joe came outside; he had a grim look on his face; the jazz musician asked him what was wrong. Joe explained that even though it felt good to have his dream come true, success didn't feel like he thought it would. He thought it would feel different in his mind, which translated to better. The saxophone player told Soul it was like a proverb where a fish was looking for the ocean, and the older fish said to him they were in it. The smaller fish explained that the sea is not always gigantic. We might be already in the ocean but not recognize it because we expect it to feel different.

The day I graduated with my bachelor's degree, I thought I'd feel complete, but I cried salty tears on the big brown envelope when the degree came in the mail. I expected to feel different. I thought it was the answer to all my problems. My elders implanted into me to get my education, so in my mind, once I got the degree, it would somehow "fix" me. All the work I'd done, that piece of paper didn't fix me. I still had internal work to do.

Five years went by before I went back to school again. Yes, I'd taken some shorter courses for the military. But to enroll in college to do all that work only to feel let down again was too much; I wasn't ready. Along the way, someone told me not to pursue my master's degree until I knew what I wanted to be when I grew up. It took five years, but I was excited when I started my master's degree. I knew this was it—no more school. I had zero desire to acquire a Ph.D, and I also knew I did not want to spend my retirement going to school. So, I started my master's degree in February 2018.

Wanna know a secret? I thought about quitting a lot; I pondered why I started another degree. Was it really for me? Or was I doing it for my grandmother again? What if I completed my degree and couldn't find a job in my desired field when I retired? What if I finished my degree and then figured out that I want to pursue a different career?

Periods of self-doubt entered my mind mid-way through each class I took. But I finished. I graduated. My grandmother sat through my virtual ceremony and took a screenshot of my face when my picture popped up on the screen. She was proud, my co-workers were proud, my kids were proud, and I was proud too. I did not have the feelings of despair I experienced when I finished my bachelor's. This time, my achievement was for me.

PERSPECTIVE

While achieving the degree was still not the ultimate high point in my life, it felt damn good to know I'd exhausted all my educational benefits, which was why I entered the military. So, am I fixed? Not by a long shot, but I am in a better place than where I was twenty-two years ago. And while the degrees are nice, somewhere along the way, I found myself. I discovered I enjoy teaching others. I love helping adults who want to seek self-improvement. Doing that work along with writing is my passion. Both allow me to tap into my creative side. The best part of my profession and passion is that they are only for me.

TOOLS THAT HELPED ME

To find my light, I first had to visualize where I saw myself at the end. Before I started my master's degree, someone told me that before I picked a major to think of the end goal in my mind and work backward. So, I started to look at job postings offering the salary I wanted to make, and I looked at the types of degrees required and worked backward. It's the same with finding your light.

Where do you see yourself? You must allow yourself to remove all your mental blocks and dream. If money and your current circumstances weren't a barrier, what would you do? Where would you live, what would you drive? Where would you work or volunteer every day? Take out a pen and answer those questions. You need to close your eyes and see it and use all your senses to feel it. If it doesn't make your heart skip a beat, put it to the side. You also need to be a little selfish and make sure what your doing is for you.

Don't pick something that fits your cultural norms. Don't pick something that will make your family happy. Don't copy somebody else. Make sure it's only for you. Once you've painted the picture in your mind, write it down. Use what you want as your driver every day. Anytime past behaviors hurt or get in your way, look at what you wrote down and keep moving forward.

Silence the negative internal voices, remember you are your own worst enemy. Tell the naysayers, including yourself, to shut up. Lastly, don't be afraid to shed the protective actions you've used to help you survive trauma. Once you can overcome harmful practices and behaviors, you might find a version of yourself hiding underneath that's better than the old you've been hiding.

The puzzle that is you continues to take shape as you grow and change. Maybe it doesn't match the picture on the front of the box, but you know something? It doesn't have to. Gather the pieces of your puzzle. Get rid out the ones that no longer suit you. Cherish the ones that do and when the frame no longer fits, toss the whole thing out and start again with new hopes and dreams.

The best stories, the ones that matter, always start that way.

Yvonne Elliott

was born and raised on the west side of Chicago Illinois. She started writing poetry at a young age as a way to process the world around her. She's an Air Force veteran with twenty-two years of military experience. When she isn't writing, you can find her relaxing at home with her husband and two children, out in her garden, or traveling with friends. Rebirth Rising out of the Shadows and into Your Own light is her first book.

Website: https://authoryvonneelliott.com
Socialtap: https://socialtap.us/AuthorYvonneElliott/
Email: AuthorYvonneElliott@gmail.com